ALONG THE
WAY

VIBRANT
BOOKS

JOSIAH SMITH

ALONG THE WAY

A BEGINNER'S GUIDE
TO JOURNEYING WITH
JESUS IN THE KINGDOM

General Director of Publications: David W. Ray
Managing Editor of Publications: Lance Colkmire
Layout: Michael McDonald
Cover design: Joshua Watts
Printed in the United States of America

ISBN 978-1-64288-078-6

**VIBRANT
BOOKS**

Visit *www.pathwaypress.org* for more information.

Dedicated to the family that is
New Hope Community Church.
Love you guys!

Table of Contents

Preface

Whether you are a believer in Jesus or not, whether you belong to a local church or prefer to go it alone, or whether you're a seasoned saint or a beginner in the way of Jesus, I'm glad you have this book.

The book you hold started as a simple tool for the local church I pastor, New Hope Community Church. We have a goal for everyone in our church to be in a mentoring relationship. This means that every person is walking with another person helping and being helped in their journey with Jesus. My team and I started meeting one-on-one with those who were new believers or new to the church. As we did, I began to write material that I felt would cover the "essentials" of the Christian faith to use in these coaching moments. I had no idea how difficult that would be! After writing and rewriting, I realized it would be easier for each individual to have their own book to read and write in. Thus began the journey to write and publish what you are now reading.

I want to encourage you not to read this book alone. This book consists of seven parts, each made up of several two- to three-page chapters. It was written with the hope that one would read the chapters and, at the end of each section, meet with a peer or mentor to review and discuss what was read. Find someone to coach, be coached by, or simply find a friend with whom you can discuss the material. The idea of coaching or mentoring may appear scary to some but it really just means sharing what you have. It means walking through life together. Find someone whom you admire and learn from them. Find someone who is going where you've already been and share your journey. Everyone has something to learn and everyone has something to share. In this way, a relationship is formed and the expectation is set that walking with Jesus is meant to be a communal experience.

Together, you can discuss the chapter themes by (1) reviewing the questions at the end of each chapter and (2) completing the application exercise that concludes each part. These are meant to help you think through and apply the concepts you encounter so you are set up to continue a life of discipleship as you walk with others. As an old African proverb goes, "If you want to go fast, go alone. If you want to go far, go together."

As you read and discuss the material, may you come to know and experience the Kingdom way of life that God intends for you. In John 10:10, Jesus said He came so you might have life, and have it to the full. So find a partner and let's dive right in!

Introduction

First things first. Let's talk a little bit about you.

You have a story. You are not an accident, nor are you a small blip on the radar. You are a custom-crafted creation and have been handpicked for a specific purpose by the God of the universe! He says you're a big deal. Think back over your life for a moment. Each day, seemingly significant or not, has been joined together by God to create the life you are currently living. Every relationship, every celebratory season, every disappointment, every mistake—all of it has added something to your story. And while not everything in your life has been good up to this point, God wants to use it in such a way that it turns out for your good. God is a specialist in finding unlikely people in overlooked places and using them to do extraordinary things. He wants to use His power on your behalf to write your story so it is for your good and ultimately brings Him glory.

However, in this process of coming to understand your story, it is important to realize from the get-go that your story isn't actually about you. That's right, your story is not *about* you; and, ultimately, it's not *for* you either. Your story is vitally important and desperately needs to be told, but it only makes sense when joined with another story—a story that has been unfolding since the dawn of creation and is still being written. This may be hard to believe when you're caught in the thick of things, just trying to make ends meet day to day—working overtime, washing dishes, paying bills, taking kids to school, and sorting out relationships, but each moment of your life is part of a grand story that intertwines the rich and the poor, the old and the young, the hidden and the famous, and everyone in between throughout all of history! Apart from this larger story your life won't make sense, and without your personal life story in the mix this greater epic is incomplete.

This great story is God's story. It's the story of a Creator and His creation, of a Father and His children, of the God of the universe making a way for you, your family, your neighbors, and every person in every corner of the earth to be in relationship with Himself. It's the story of the Kingdom. It's the story of relationship, of training for war and learning to follow, of discovery, and of partnering with God to see His purposes fulfilled in our lives and in our world.

Are you up for the story? As you read, may you discover the joy of journeying with King Jesus and may these few pages simply help you along the way.

PART ONE:
The Story of a Kingdom

*From that time Jesus began to preach, saying,
"Repent, for the kingdom of heaven is at hand."*
(Matthew 4:17)

1
The Kingdom at Creation

Do you remember the movie *The Princess Diaries*? In this movie, Anne Hathaway plays Mia Thermopolis, a regular girl awkwardly making her way through high school, trying to figure out where she belongs, crushing on boys—until one day she abruptly discovers that she is actually a real-life princess and heir to the throne of a small European principality called Genovia. This shocking truth has a profound impact on her life as she comically moves from living a "normal" teenage life to learning what it means to live as royalty.

You and I have a lot in common with Mia Thermopolis. You might think of yourself as a fairly normal person. You go to school or work, you write papers and get projects done, you go home, you eat, and you sleep; and then you wake up to do it all over again. But what you may not realize is that you are destined for greatness! God, in all His wisdom, has made a Kingdom and has given you a very important part to play in it. You are not a nobody and you are not just anybody; you were created to be a royal son or daughter of the King! Maybe this all sounds a bit far-fetched and a little too fantastic, but God desires for you to realize your royal identity so you can live life as He intends. He wants to lead you on a journey to discover His kingdom and walk in this new identity as His child.

You see, God never intended for us to get caught up in dead religious activity; instead, He made us to thrive as we fulfill a role in His Kingdom. At the beginning of time, when God created the heavens and the earth, He established a kingdom. By definition, a *kingdom* is a "place of dominion." It is an area over which someone holds authority. God the Creator is King and creation His domain. While God ruled over everything before He created anything, and of course rules over what He has created, He never intended to reign alone. Rather, He created mankind to rule with Him. Genesis 1:27-28 tells us:

> So God created human beings in his own image. In the image of God he created them; male and female he created them.
> Then God blessed them and said, "Be fruitful and multiply. Fill the earth and govern it. Reign over the fish in the sea, the birds in the sky, and all the animals that scurry along the ground" (NLT).

In the beginning, God gave Adam and Eve dominion over the earth and everything in it. They were God's established rulers with authority to oversee the planet. They lived in perfect relationship with their Creator-King and lacked nothing. There was no pain, no suffering, no loneliness, no tears—all was as it should be under God's reign.

– Questions to Consider –

• What would change about your life if you found you belonged to a royal family?

• What are some elements you think of when you hear the word *kingdom*? How does a kingdom differ from other forms of government (democracy, dictatorship, etc.)?

2
The Disastrous Fall & Analogous Law

There was trouble in paradise. Though all was perfect for a while, one of God's created beings, an angel, attempted to usurp the throne. Being no match at all for God, he was banished from Heaven and made to roam the earth. This angelic adversary came and tempted Adam and Eve to disobey God and choose their way over His, ignorant self-rule instead of loving submission to God's good order. This was the very first sin, which brought Adam and Eve into a disastrous power struggle against God—a trait they have passed down through all generations right up to the present. Like oil and water, sin and holiness cannot coexist. So Adam and Eve were displaced from their perfect home, and because the ugly effects of sin always reach farther than bargained for, even the earth itself became a place of toil and struggle rather than joy and peace.

This God-opposition, creating separation between mankind and their Maker, was exactly what *the satan* (which literally means "accuser" or "adversary") had wanted. Having launched his rebellion, Satan now became overseer of earth's domain, and evil became the world's default. But our God knows no surprise, and sin entering the world was no exception. He already had a plan. In the first phase of this glorious plan of restoration, He would need to reveal the damaging effects of rebellion. As a loving father corrects his erring child, God would expose sin's consequence and provide a better way.

Hundreds of years after Adam and Eve's failure, God chose a man named Abraham and called him to leave his house, extended family, and homeland to embark on a journey into the unknown. Abraham followed God not knowing where he was going but believing that God had something better for him than what he could plan for himself (Hebrews 11:8-10). Through Abraham, God raised up a people group called "Israel" to be set apart as His very own. God made a *covenant* (an unbreakable promise) with them that He would be their God and they would be His people. He gave them a way to live called the "Law" as well as leaders called prophets and judges to help ensure they stayed on the right path. God was showing the rest of the world what it looked like to live in His Kingdom. Through the Law He taught Israel the right way to live and, through a system of offerings and sacrifices, He provided a way to temporarily pardon the many times they failed to live accordingly.

Since the consequence of breaking this Law was death, God allowed the people to kill animals as a way to pay for the sins they were committing. The problem with covering sin through animal sacrifice was that it never made sin go away; it merely postponed the deadly consequences until the next sacrifice was made. This system of "sin payments" covered the symptoms but never dealt with the root issue, the seed of sin that is born in the human heart. Instead, it magnified people's inability to live "righteously"—in right relationship with God and according to His standard (Romans 5:20).

Israel continually failed to live rightly and so failed to accurately represent God's Kingdom to the world. God sent messengers to correct and guide Israel and patiently provided multiple "second" chances, but the people's hearts never changed. They were a kingdom on earth, but they never accurately represented how God's Kingdom was to function. Through Israel's failure to live God's way, the world saw how deep the sin issue went. No one could attain the perfect life that relationship with a perfect God required. And since sin had affected everyone, no one was in a place to eliminate the sin debt. Instead of living as God's royal ones, humankind was relegated to living as slaves, following the orders of their own sinful desires (Romans 6:16).

Despite the gloomy picture, God had not made a mistake. This too had been thought of in God's plan, and what was to happen next would change the world forever. When the time was just right, He would send His own Son, Jesus, into the everyday dirt and grime of creation to take care of the sin problem once and for all, and make a way for all people to be in relationship with their Creator once more.

− Questions to Consider −

• What are some of the disastrous effects sin has had on the world?

• The Bible calls the Law a "teacher" (see Galatians 3:24-26). What does the Law teach us? How does the Law point us to our need for Jesus?

3
The Kingdom Restored

Enslaved for four hundred years, divinely delivered from slavery, nationalized as a great kingdom, devastatingly conquered and ransacked, taken to live in a foreign land, and gathered back to their homeland, the people of Israel now suffered under the iron rule of the Roman Empire. No longer a nation of their own and under the close watch of Rome, the Jewish people longed for a heroic, kingly leader to rise up and overthrow their oppressors so Israel could again be established as a kingdom of the earth. They anticipated it.

Centuries before, God had promised David, Israel's greatest king, that he would have a descendant who would rule and reign as king forever (2 Samuel 7:12-16). The nation's prophets had predicted the birth of the One who would save them. There would be a *Messiah*, the "Anointed One," who would set the captives free and usher in the time of God's favor (Isaiah 61:1-3). He would be a light for the world and bring justice not only to Israel but to all nations (42:1-7). Israel eagerly awaited the day their king would come and save them from their sorrow and suffering.

Enter Jesus. Born in poverty, raised in obscurity, and living humbly, no one thought this man could be their king. No one expected this man to be their God. Jesus claimed to be both. As Jesus went from town to town, He proclaimed, "Repent, for the Kingdom of Heaven is at hand" (Matthew 4:17). He spoke with authority, healing the sick and casting out demons, and taught with heavenly wisdom. He lived free of fear and worry, instead offering peace, joy, hope, and healing to all who came to Him. He lived outside the oppressive weight of religion no one else could escape. He modeled Kingdom life by welcoming God's heavenly power into earthly situations. He spoke of God as His Father and lived in perfect submission and obedience to His Father's will. Following the heart of God in every moment of His life, Jesus never once rebelled in sin. Truly, Jesus showed us what it looks like to live under God's reign on earth.

From the start, Jesus knew He was sent for a purpose: to restore men and women to their intended place in God's Kingdom. He wanted to move people out of a life enslaved to sin into a life marked by friendship with God. To do this, He would need to settle the sin issue. He would need to make a once-and-for-all payment for all people's sinfulness. That is why, after 33 years of living as a man in perfect relationship with the Father, Jesus gave Himself up to suffer the sentence of a rebel—crucifixion. He was the perfect sacrifice to which the Law had pointed. By giving His life, He paid for our debt of sin and all its effects—shame, guilt, disease, and death—He covered it all! Three days after His death by crucifixion, Jesus revealed His conquest over death itself and rose from the grave. In doing so, He stripped Satan of all authority and sealed his fate of defeat.

Now humankind could live free once more! No longer would people have to be enslaved to sin; we could live as sons and daughters of the King. Jesus paid the debt for sin we were unable to pay. Now, rather than us striving in vain trying to be good enough for a perfect God and hoping to please Him in our efforts, Jesus made a way for us to be freely cleansed of all sin and its disastrous effects and to live as righteous children of God (2 Corinthians 5:21). In His mercy He spared us from death, and in His kindness, He gave us life. Through faith in Jesus' divine exchange, we could once more live in right relationship with God, our Father. God's Kingdom had been restored to humankind.

– Questions to Consider –

• What was Jesus' purpose in coming to earth? (See Luke 19:10; John 3:16-17; 10:10; 1 Timothy 1:15.)

• How is having faith in Jesus different than merely being a good person?

4
The Kingdom Within Us

The Kingdom of God did not retreat from earth when Jesus ascended back to Heaven. Jesus had a plan for Kingdom expansion that would continue far beyond His earthly life. In John 14:12, Jesus told His disciples that whoever believes in Him would not only do the works that He did, but they would do even greater works. Just a few verses later, Jesus gave insight into how that would be possible: He would send a Helper who would remain with them forever—the Spirit of God Himself, the Holy Spirit.

While Jesus was on earth, He taught His disciples to do the same works He did. He taught His disciples to pray, "Our Father in Heaven . . . Your Kingdom come, Your will be done, on earth as it is in Heaven." He sent His disciples out to heal the sick, cast out demons, and proclaim the reality of God's Kingdom everywhere. Now, having returned to His heavenly throne, Jesus has given Kingdom authority to His Church. Empowered by the Holy Spirit, disciples from the early church in the Book of Acts all the way to the global Church of today have been God's avenue of making His Kingdom known in the earth.

While it may be tempting to think this is just a fairy tale and should be left for the theological "pros" or heroes of the Bible, Jesus has called each of us to live Kingdom lives just as He did. You may feel a bit nervous at the thought of living as Jesus did, speaking in authority and casting out demons and healing the sick, but what you must know is that the Kingdom is within *you*! You are an ambassador of the Kingdom (2 Corinthians 5:20). Whenever a kingdom sends out a representative, that person is sent in the name of the king. She does not go of her own accord or in her own authority. She goes with the weight of the kingdom behind her. The king's army, the king's treasury, and all the resources of the kingdom are available to her as long as she is representing the king.

The same is true for us as representatives of Jesus. When we go in Jesus' name, all of Heaven is backing us. We walk in Christ's authority. We go with God's provision. We have nothing to worry about and nothing to fear. God has given us all we need to live this Jesus life. It is our responsibility simply to follow and obey. As we listen, God reveals to us His identity as our loving Father-King and our identity as children and royal ambassadors. As we walk in obedience, the domain of darkness is pushed back and earth reflects Heaven more and more.

– Questions to Consider –

• What kind of works did Jesus do while here on earth?

• How would you act differently if you believed you were a representative of King Jesus?

5
The Kingdom in Fullness

We now live in the tension between two worlds: God's heavenly Kingdom and this present darkness that still calls earth its home. While Satan has ultimately been defeated and stripped of his authority, sin and evil still abound. Satan still roams the earth trying to wreak havoc. The earth remains under the power of sin's curse. Picture the earth covered by a giant dome of darkness, separating it from the heavens above. This is the case with our sinful world, separated from Heaven and living under the shadow of sin.

Under sin's mastery, we miss out on Heaven's blessings. We do not see God for who He is. We live without His favor. We live burdened by the weight of sin. But Jesus came, and through His life, death, and resurrection, He broke through this dome of darkness. He bridged the gap between a holy Heaven and a sinful earth and made God's glory available to those previously "stuck" under the dome. Jesus shined His light into the darkness and made it possible for us to see and experience God's glory and truth by believing in Him (John 8:12; Isaiah 60:1-3).

Not only has Jesus enabled us to see, the apostle Paul tells us in his letter to the Ephesians that God has "raised us up with Him and seated us with Him in the heavenly places in Christ Jesus" (2:1-10). In essence, Jesus has pierced through the darkness, letting His light shine through, and has pulled us out and invited us to sit with Him at His throne. If we have repented of our sins and have accepted this glorious invitation, we now live a dual reality: physically, we are still present here on the earth with all its pain and problems; but spiritually, we sit with Christ in Heaven and gain His perspective. We live on earth, but we also live above the dome.

God's ultimate goal is for earth to resemble Heaven once more. While darkness continues to blanket our world, Christ's light can be seen shining through. John's recording of the Gospel says Jesus' light "shines in the darkness, and the darkness can never extinguish it" (1:5 NLT). As a matter of fact, God's light isn't just enduring, it is ever increasing in our world! Though we presently live in the tension of two realms, the time is coming when darkness will be completely destroyed, and only God's Kingdom will remain. One day, when the Good News of Jesus has been preached around the world, the end will come and Jesus will return to earth again to complete what He started (Matthew 24:14). This time He won't just break through the dome—He will completely destroy it. Satan, the accuser, will be cast out from the earth along with evil and all who rejected Jesus' offer of life. And then all things will be made new. God will recreate Heaven and earth in perfection and glory.

Revelation 21 paints a beautiful picture of Heaven coming down and God making His home on earth present with His people. There will be no more death, no more pain or mourning, no more sin or its evil effects (v. 5). All will be well when the Kingdom comes in fullness. Until then, Jesus has sent us out to the world to point people to His light and to offer the life and freedom that can only be found in Him.

– Questions to Consider –

• Is life still difficult after you've submitted your life to Jesus? Why or why not?

• How does knowing the Kingdom is coming in fullness affect your current way of living (see Titus 2:11-14; 1 Peter 4:1-11)?

– Application Exercise –
Creating a Life Map

A life map is a simple way to consider the story arch of your life—where you've been and where you are headed. You can do this by reviewing significant events in your life, both happy and sad, and putting them on paper. There are many ways to create a life map. Talk with your coach or simply google "create a life map" to learn more. Construct a life map this week to help you consider how God has been at work in your life and how He may be using your story to be part of the larger story of the Kingdom.

PART TWO:
It's About Relationship

"You are to love the Lord Yahweh, your God, with every passion of your heart, with all the energy of your being, with every thought that is within you, and with all your strength."
(Mark 12:30 TPT)

6
Dethroning Self

God is not robotic nor does He desire robots to serve Him. In wisdom, God has made it so everything in His Kingdom functions and flows within the context of relationship. He does not want religious machines pre-programmed for mindless obedience; He wants to be in genuine and dynamic relationship with His people. The journey of a Christ-follower is that of a life moved from being an enemy of God to being a friend and family member.

We start out as God's enemy. In a kingdom, there can only be one king, and those who oppose the king's rule are enemies of the king. A kingdom is not a democracy where the majority rules, or an oligarchy where a few important people rule. It is a monarchy. Only one person rules— that person is king. When we choose to live in sin, we set ourselves up in direct opposition to the King. We not only oppose the King—in our rebellious state we try to steal God's throne. Rather than follow His way, we attempt to make our own way. Rather than trust His loving care, we rely on ourselves and try to live a self-made life.

An easy way to discover who sits on the throne of our heart is to ask, *Who has the final say in my life? What determines how I make decisions?* For some it is their closest friends or their peer group. For others, their public persona or reputation guides their decisions. All of these and more really boil down to "king self" being on the throne. A person enters the Kingdom when he or she in essence has said, "I don't want to—I can't—play the part of king anymore. I recognize Jesus as the one true King and give Him His rightful place in my life." Self is dethroned, and we have chosen to submit to the rule and reign of Jesus. Without an understanding of this central concept, no other kingdom concept matters. This is foundational. If you insist on being the king of your life, then Jesus cannot be your king.

Whether we like to admit it or not, we all fight to maintain a sense of control over our lives. It gives us a sort of false security, thinking we know best and can dictate the outcome of the good and bad in our lives as long as we are in charge. The Bible talks a lot about this idea and much of life revolves around this issue. In Luke 9:23-24, Jesus told His followers:

> If anyone would come after Me, he must deny himself, and take up his cross daily and follow Me. For whoever would save his life will lose it, but whoever loses his life for My sake will save it.

To live we must die. To find our life we must lose it. It seems a bit backwards, but this same idea is reflected in nature. Jesus used the analogy of a seed to explain this: "Unless a grain of wheat falls into the earth and dies, it remains alone; but if it dies, it bears much fruit" (John 12:24). A tree cannot grow where a seed refuses to die. But where a seed does die it is transformed, eventually becoming a beautiful place of shelter and rest.

When we give up the right to rule and choose to follow Jesus, we are transformed from enemy to friend. We find that the King we resisted all along had actually been fighting *for* us. We were in rebellion, and He was simply after our hearts. Acknowledging His place as King, we understand His great mercy and are invited into friendship with God.

– Questions to Consider –

*Marriage
+
Ministry*

• What are some areas you need to surrender for Jesus to have complete reign in your life? *DAILY SURRENDER*

• Study the illustration below (from *cru.org*). Would you say you are living a self-directed life or a Christ-directed life?

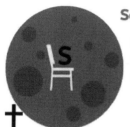

Self-Directed Life

S Self is on the throne

† Christ is outside the life

● Interests are directed by the self, often resulting in discord and frustration.

Christ-Directed Life

† Christ is on the throne

S Self is yielding to Christ

● Interests are directed by Christ, resulting in harmony with God'd plan.

7
Made for Relationship

When we choose to follow Jesus and give Him full access to our lives, allowing Him the authority in our lives that is rightfully His, a wonderful thing happens: we are adopted into His family and His life springs up in us. In Galatians 2:20, the apostle Paul says:

> I have been crucified with Christ. It is no longer I who live, but Christ who lives in me. And the life I now live in the flesh I live by faith in the Son of God, who loved me and gave Himself for me.

Paul found that when he died to self, Christ's life was formed in Him. When Christ is formed in us, we become free to follow. We are no longer enslaved by sin, having to carry out selfish and sinful desires, but are unshackled to follow King Jesus—to live and learn His way (Romans 6:6-12). Now free from sin, we are brought into God's family where God is not just King, but our Father; and knowing Him is not a set of religious rules, but a relationship.

Like human relationships, friendship with God is a wonderful, ongoing process of love and discovery. It means spending time together, discovering the likes and dislikes of one another, practicing healthy communication, and building trust. It requires investment and carries a precious return: intimacy—knowing and being known. (Some describe *intimacy* as "into me you see.") Throughout Scripture, God reveals Himself through a number of relational terms. God reveals Himself as Husband, Friend, Shepherd, and more (Isaiah 54:5; John 15:15; Psalm 23). But the primary way God has revealed Himself relationally is as Father. Throughout Jesus' time on earth, He almost exclusively refers to God as "Father." You may be tempted to think this title was reserved for Jesus' use, but in Matthew 6:9, when teaching His disciples to pray, Jesus taught them to say, "Our Father in Heaven. . . ." He did not just say, *My Father*—He intended for us to come into this understanding, too, by saying, "*Our* Father."

While some of us may have had negative experiences with our earthly fathers, God is not a reflection of our shortcomings. He is a good Father who loves His children faultlessly. He cares for us, provides for us, and loves us perfectly. James 1:17 says everything good in our lives comes from God. In Matthew 7:7-11, Jesus reminds us of how good a Father God is through analogy:

> Ask, and it will be given to you; seek, and you will find; knock, and it will be opened to you. For everyone who asks receives, and the one who seeks finds, and to the one who knocks it will be opened. Or which one of you, if his son asks him for bread, will give him a stone? Or if he asks for a fish, will give him a serpent? If you then, who are evil, know how to give good gifts to your children, how much more will your Father who is in heaven give good things to those who ask him!

In Galatians 4:6-7, Paul tells us we are now children of God who get to call out to Him, "Abba, Father." *Abba* means "daddy." It's an intimate term between child and father. How incredible that the God of the universe would choose to relate to us in this way!! Once enemies, now friends. Once orphans, now sons and daughters.

— Questions to Consider —

• What are the qualities of a good relationship? Have these qualities been present in your relationship with God? Why or why not?

• Is the idea that God is a good Father easy or difficult to believe? Why? How might viewing God as "Papa" change the way you relate to God?

8
Communicating with God

Imagine a relationship without any communication. It wouldn't be much of a relationship! As we come to know God, we should expect to communicate with Him. That doesn't just mean talking *at* Him. It means talking *with* Him, which includes hearing *from* Him. John 10:4 tells us that as God's people we hear His voice. We hear and we follow. God is not sitting silently in the sky, observing our lives but never interacting with us—He is interested in our everyday lives! He knows the moment we wake and is with us as we sleep. He hears every prayer we pray before a word is on our tongue (Psalm 139:4). God not only loves to hear our prayers, He also loves to answer them (1 John 5:14-15). He is not holding out on us. He is eager to speak with us. While most of us never hear a big, booming voice from the sky, God does speak to us, using a variety of means to get our attention. A few ways by which you can expect to hear from God as you journey in relationship with Him are the Bible, Holy Spirit, godly counsel, and signs.

The Bible

One of the surest ways to know God has spoken and is speaking to us is through the Bible. The Bible is a written compilation of God's words and the story of God and humankind. What God spoke in the Bible still rings true today (Psalm 119:89; Matthew 24:35; Numbers 23:19). By reading and living according to Scripture we learn of who God is and how He speaks. The more we obey Scripture the more we will understand God's ways and God's voice. Second Timothy 3:16 tells us all Scripture is inspired by God and is useful to teach us what is true and to make us realize what is wrong in our lives. It corrects us when we are wrong and teaches us to do what is right.

As we read the Bible, God will speak to us about areas of our lives that need to change. He may also correct a thought pattern that does not align with His heart. He will show us what is right and teach us how to get there (Hebrews 4:12; James 1:23; Psalm 119).

Holy Spirit

God also speaks to us through what we might call "inner impressions." God is Spirit and He speaks to us internally to our spirit, our "inner man." Perhaps as we are praying or maybe in response to something someone says or something we read, we get a feeling in our "gut." Maybe a word or a picture pops up in our mind. This is one way God speaks to us. It is His Spirit speaking to our spirit. You may have experienced this when you first committed your life to Jesus. You sensed the Holy Spirit convicting you of sin and calling you to Himself. Perhaps it simply came as an overwhelming feeling, but you knew God was speaking to you. The important thing to remember is that God never contradicts what He has already spoken. What He says may not always make sense to our human intellect, but it will always align with what has been revealed in the Bible.

Godly Counsel

Another way God speaks to us is through godly counsel— advice given from a mature believer or group of believers. It is important to have friends and advisors in your life who have experience following Jesus and can offer godly wisdom for your situation. Proverbs 12:15 says, "The way of a fool is right in his own eyes, but a wise man listens to advice." Everyone needs wise counsel. This is one of the reasons it is so important to be involved in a Christian community. Wise counsel may come through a teaching in a church service, in a discussion with a Bible-study group, or from someone you have asked to walk with you and give you guidance. When godly advisors speak into your life, be sure to pay attention to what they are saying and ask God to confirm what they are saying through Scripture and the Holy Spirit.

Signs

A sign is simply something that shows the way and gives direction. If we are open to it, God often speaks to us through life's everyday circumstances. A sign from God could be an experience or word spoken to you several times in a short period of time. It could be an encouraging or directive word spoken to you by someone with the gift of prophecy (to be discussed in a future chapter). You may have a dream that carries a deeper meaning.[1] A window of opportunity may arise or suddenly be dismissed. These signs don't always come in a big billboard fashion, but as we seek God He is faithful to reveal Himself and His will and to give direction. Our focus must simply be on knowing Him and doing His will. He will confirm His word with signs that align with His Spirit and what is written in the Bible.

– Questions to Consider –

• In what ways has God spoken to you in the past?

• What are some ways we can test whether or not what we are hearing is from God?

---

[1] In the Bible we see God speak to people through dreams as they sleep or in visions when they are awake. The basic concept of a dream or vision from God is that He speaks to you through a picture, a scene, or a similar "movie" of the mind. Ask your coach or pastor for further clarity on this topic.

9
Love's Response

The beauty of relationship is that it takes two. It's a team effort. Relationship forms when one person takes the risk to initiate and the other responds. It may start as a nervous "hello" that leads to exchanging phone numbers that later leads to a first date which could eventually result in a commitment that develops into an "I love you." Or it may start with a "hello" and end right there. Relationships depend on both initiation and response. With no initiation there can be no response. With no response there can be no relationship.

This may be a scary prospect to consider for the one initiating because there is the real possibility of being rejected. However, in relationship with God we never have to fear because He always initiates—and He does not fear being rejected. He pursues unwaveringly!

God initiated relationship with us by sending Jesus to live and die as the once-and-for-all payment for our sin so nothing would stand between us. Restored to right relationship with God, we hear His voice and receive greater understanding into who He is and what He is like and what He desires. He continues pursuing, inviting us ever deeper into relationship. This brings us to moments of decision. We must choose how we will respond to this deeper understanding of God and His way. Will we listen to truth, trust His directives, and draw nearer to Him? Or will we, in fear, reject this knowledge and distance ourselves from our Father-King?

The way we respond to God reveals the desires of our hearts. The apostle John tells us if we love God we will obey Him. If we don't obey Him, His love has not been made perfect in us (1 John 2:4-5). This indicates that *an obedience problem is a love problem*. Any time we stubbornly choose our own way rather than His, we need to check the throne of our heart and ask God to reveal what it is we are loving more than Him. Then, we need to align our thoughts, attitudes, and actions with His heart and trust His loving intentions for us.

As we hear from God and respond to Him, we move deeper into relationship. The more we respond with a "yes" to God, the more we know and love Him. The more we know and love Him, the more we are able to accurately discern what He is saying; do you see the pattern? Just as with human relationships, walking with God is a process. We don't come to know a person in a day. Learning to know someone's voice and character is developed over a lifetime. It requires discussion and discovery to find out what they like and dislike. It requires shared experiences to deepen trust and intimacy. It requires an intentional choice to keep loving no matter what. It comes with a fair share of mistakes and takes time.

As we continue in this lifelong relational process, we find that our King is a faithful Friend and Father whose love will never, ever fail. Yes, it is up to us to respond. But when, drawn by His kindness, we come to encounter this relentless God, we grow in love and overcome fear. We are freed to delve deeper into a trusting relationship with our loving God. This then leads to greater revelation which again calls for response, leading us deeper still into loving relationship. And so the journey, full of challenges and discoveries, grows sweeter and sweeter to the end.

– Questions to Consider –

• How have you said "yes" to Jesus? How have you said "no"? What impact did these differing responses have on your relationship with God?

• How are love and obedience related (see John 14:15)? Where do love and obedience fit in the picture below?

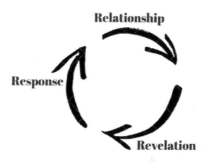

– Application Exercise –
Letter to a Friend

Write a letter to God about where you are in your relationship with Him and where you would like to see the relationship go. Write as you would to a close friend. To take the exercise a step further, write a second letter, this time from God's perspective to you.

PART THREE:
Our Faithful Guide

"When the Spirit of truth comes, he will guide you into all truth, for he will not speak on his own authority, but whatever he hears he will speak, and he will declare to you the things that are to come. He will glorify me, for he will take what is mine and declare it to you."
(John 16:13-14)

10
Sent to Help

Have you ever found yourself lost on a windy back road because you refused to ask for directions? Yikes! Trying to find the way without help can quickly get you lost, frustrated, and confused. That's why it is so important to have someone to train and to guide you when embarking on a difficult or dangerous venture. Soldiers have commanding officers, athletes have personal trainers, and travelers have tour guides. We all need someone to lead the way and instruct us as we go. Thankfully, Jesus our King has not left us alone on this journey of life. Nor has He left us helpless in our battle against darkness. He has given us a Helper along the way—our own personal trainer and faithful guide.

As Jesus was nearing His miraculous departure from earth, He told His disciples that He was going to send someone to them who would continue to teach them and be their guide. He would give them the Helper who would enable them to carry out His mission of bringing the Kingdom of Heaven to earth. This "someone" was the Holy Spirit.

Today, many people live in a cloud of mystery and confusion when it comes to the Holy Spirit. We've heard about Him and may even confess belief in Him as part of a doctrinal statement, but many have never really taken the time to get to know Him. What a tragedy that we would have such a good guide and never even know who He is!

First, the Holy Spirit is a person. He is not a mystical idea or an impersonal, Star Wars-like force. The Holy Spirit is a real and active person who wants to engage in a living and active relationship with us. The Bible consistently shows the Holy Spirit communicating and participating in the lives of normal people like you and me.

Second, the Bible reveals the Holy Spirit is God himself. In John 14:16, Jesus says, "I will ask the Father, and he will give you another Helper, to be with you forever." The "Helper" Jesus was referring to is the Holy Spirit. The word "another" implies this is *another of the same kind*" (see Bill Johnson's *God Is Good* to learn more.) The Father sent Jesus, the Son, who is one with the Father. Now the Father is sending "another of the same kind," the Holy Spirit. Some Christians treat the Holy Spirit as less divine than God the Father or Jesus the Son, but the Holy Spirit is as equally God as the Father and the Son. This is the beauty and complexity of what we call the Holy Trinity: God, three distinct persons yet one.

Third, the Holy Spirit has been sent to help us live as Jesus lived. Just like God the Father and God the Son, the Holy Spirit has a specific role to carry out. As quoted above, the Holy Spirit is called our Helper. This word can also be translated "Advocate," "Counselor," or "Comforter." He works on our behalf, instructing us and reminding us of the words of Jesus. The Holy Spirit continues the ministry of Jesus and directs all attention to Him (see John 15:26-27; 16:12-15). The Holy Spirit, also called "the Spirit of truth," shows us the right path to walk and helps us in time of need. When we don't know what to do, the Holy Spirit prays for us and guides us in the Father's will (Romans 8:26-27). Truly, the Holy Spirit is the best guide we could have. Let's get to know Him!

– Questions to Consider –

• What comes to mind when you think about the Holy Spirit?

• In what ways does the Holy Spirit help us?

11
Here to Stay

The Holy Spirit has been at work since before the beginning of time. Like Jesus and the Father, He existed before anything was made and participated in creating all that now exists (Genesis 1:2). Throughout the Old Testament the Holy Spirit is seen at work empowering specific people for specific works of service and miraculous feats. By the Spirit's gifting, a man named Bezalel built the Old Testament Tabernacle (God's house, so to speak) with artistry and skill (Exodus 31:1-11). By the Spirit's power, Samson received divine strength to conquer a thousand enemy Philistines with nothing but a donkey's jawbone (Judges 13—16). By the Spirit's guidance and inspiration, men and women (including Isaiah, Jeremiah, and Joel) prophesied of future events that were impossible to know at the time and yet came to pass with detailed accuracy. The Old Testament is filled with stories of the Holy Spirit operating through chosen individuals to accomplish miraculous assignments as God showed the world what it meant to be His people.

Hundreds of years later, when Jesus came onto the scene, we start to see the Holy Spirit's role evidenced a bit more clearly. At Jesus' baptism in water, the Holy Spirit was seen descending upon Jesus like a dove and resting on Him. Before Jesus returned to Heaven, we see in John 20:22 that Jesus "breathed on [His disciples] and said to them, 'Receive the Holy Spirit.'" Following Jesus' ascension into Heaven, during a Jewish holiday called "Pentecost," we see the Holy Spirit come accompanied by the appearance of fire and the sound of a mighty wind, and empowering the 120 believers who were present at that time (Acts 2:1-4). This event was to signify that the Holy Spirit had come to stay. No longer would He rest upon an individual momentarily—He would come to live in and through all who follow Christ.

The Bible teaches the Holy Spirit lives inside of those who follow Jesus and is a seal of God's covenant with us (2 Corinthians 1:21-22; Ephesians 1:13-14; 4:30). In the days of ancient kings and kingdoms, the king had a signet ring that was used to place a seal (similar to a stamp or engraving tool) on important possessions or documents. This seal proved the authenticity of the letter or artifact and showed that it belonged to the king and carried the king's authority (we see something similar in America's presidential seal). By sealing us with His Holy Spirit, God has marked us as His own and given us His authority and approval!

The Bible also describes the Holy Spirit as a "down payment" of all God's promises, meaning we can trust all of God's promises are true and will come to pass because He has given us His Spirit as the guarantee! We don't have to wonder whether or not God is committed to us or if He will ever leave or abandon us. He has given us the assurance that He is for us. As followers of Jesus, we have God's Spirit living inside us and can be confident He is here to stay!

– Questions to Consider –

• In John 16:6-7, Jesus told His disciples it was for their own good that He go away. Why was it good for Jesus to go away?

• How does the Holy Spirit help us to know God is committed to us?

12
Power for Today

In Jesus' final words before ascending to Heaven, He told His disciples, "You will receive power when the Holy Spirit has come upon you, and you will be my witnesses in Jerusalem and in all Judea and Samaria, and to the end of the earth" (Acts 1:8). One chapter later, in Acts 2, we have the story of Pentecost. For the tenth day straight, 120 believers had gathered in an upstairs room to wait on God in prayer. As they prayed together, suddenly they heard the sound of wind rushing through the room, and something resembling fire appeared on each of them. Talk about a sight and sound experience! Next, they began to speak in languages they had never learned. The experience was so astounding that thousands gathered around to get a glimpse of what was happening. The Holy Spirit had come and filled these believers.

That day the disciples became powerful witnesses of the Gospel of Jesus Christ and proclaimed boldly that Jesus is indeed the Messiah. Peter, one of the Twelve who was closest to Jesus, preached his first "sermon," and three thousand people became believers! Before, the disciples had been hiding, locked up in a room hoping they would not be found and killed by the Jewish leaders. After receiving the Holy Spirit, they were found preaching on the streets and performing miracles in Jesus' name, unphased by prison, persecution, and even death. This small group of 120 believers quickly became a multiplying movement which turned the world as they knew it "upside down" (Acts 17:6). It may be tempting to think the Holy Spirit was only active through extra special men and women of God in Bible times. But we need to know the Holy Spirit is for us today! The story in Acts 2 of the Holy Spirit being poured out on all people was just the beginning. The Holy Spirit is presently at work in our world and wants to do the work of Jesus through us as He did through those first 120 believers.

If you have been saved and baptized in water, you should expect to be baptized in the Holy Spirit. In Acts 1:5, Jesus had told His disciples, "John baptized with water, but you will be baptized with the Holy Spirit not many days from now." The term *baptize* means "to submerge, immerse, or dip under." Depending on what faith tradition you have experienced, you may have seen someone be baptized in water by being completely dipped under water. Now Jesus is saying you won't just experience baptism as submersion in water; you'll be submersed in the Spirit of God! You too will receive the power of the Holy Spirit and will speak boldly the Good News that Jesus is alive.

Based on what we see in the Book of Acts and throughout church history, here are a few things you can expect as you seek God and experience being "baptized" or "filled" with the Holy Spirit. *You will sense the nearness of God.* The desire to thank God and praise Him will well up inside of you.

Your body may respond in some way to God's presence. This may come in the form of shaking, weeping, feeling an "electric pulse" through your body, among other sensations. *As you use your mouth to praise, you will speak words that you have previously not known.* These words will be given to you by the Spirit.

You will be filled with boldness and a supernatural zeal to tell others about the greatness of Jesus. You will be witnesses for Jesus, as He promised (Acts 1:8).

You will begin to walk in a new closeness with the Holy Spirit. What a wonderful experience! But being baptized in the Spirit isn't just about having a cool experience. The point is never just to have an experience, but to better know a Person. It is meant to introduce us to a new way of life—a life of walking with the Holy Spirit!

– Questions to Consider –

• Read Acts 2. What were the results of the disciples being filled with the Holy Spirit?

• Are you *baptized* in ("immersed, covered by") the Holy Spirit? If so, how does this affect your life?

13
Growing Good Fruit

Go to any grocery store or market and you'll see an area called "produce." This is where the fruits and veggies are—the foods that are grown from the earth. One of the defining characteristics of fruit is that they all begin as a seed. The seed develops and matures and, given time, eventually produces a ripe fruit ready for consumption. Similarly, we produce certain qualities and behaviors in and through our lives that are a result of the kinds of seeds that have been planted in us.

In his letter to the church of Galatia, the apostle Paul tells us there is "fruit" that the Spirit produces: "The fruit of the Spirit is love, joy, peace, patience, kindness, goodness, faithfulness, gentleness, self-control" (Galatians 5:22-23).

As apple seeds produce apples and blueberries produce blueberries, we can only reproduce what we are. So it is with God. He is loving, and so His Spirit produces love. He is gentle, and so His Spirit produces gentleness. Each of the nine qualities listed above are characteristics of God and His Spirit.

Here's the amazing thing: God wants to produce these same qualities in you and me! He wants our lives to produce the same kind of fruit He produces. How does He do that? Just as a seed is planted in the ground to grow, God places His Spirit in our spirit to cultivate His life in us. As we are filled with and walk daily with the Holy Spirit, the life and ways of Jesus become more and more evident in us. We are more patient when tested. We love even our enemies. We are faithful to keep our word and endure through hardship. We are able to control ourselves rather than acting out of impulse and desire. We know these are divine qualities because they don't come naturally until the Holy Spirit introduces them to us.

The way we continue to produce this fruit is by living in Christ through the Holy Spirit. Jesus compared this idea to the branches of a grapevine only producing grapes if they are connected to the vine (John 15:1-8). It's important to remember these qualities of the Holy Spirit are not produced in our lives by working harder to become good, moral people—but simply a result of being connected to Jesus. Fruit isn't grown because it tries so hard; it grows as it draws life and nourishment from its roots. One can help prepare the soil and try to ensure a proper environment for growth, but in the end fruit will grow because it's of the right seed and connected to the right root.

We cannot manufacture or earn love or joy or peace or any other divine quality in our lives. We can only give our lives to the Holy Spirit and allow Him to produce this fruit in us. You've probably heard it said that you become like those with whom you associate. The same is true of our relationship with God. As we follow His Spirit and spend time sharing our thoughts, feelings, and dreams with Him and listening for His voice, He shares His heart with us and we become more like Him. His love is formed in our hearts. His faithfulness is mirrored in our faithfulness. We grow in patience and gentleness. We are able to lead ourselves well rather than being led by our desires. God's life is produced in us.

– Questions to Consider –

• Why do you think these God-qualities are compared to fruit? How is fruit cultivated?

• Look again at Galatians 5:22-23. Which of these fruits are evident in your life? Which of these fruits do you want to be more evident in your life?

– Application Exercise –
Seeking the Holy Spirit

Spend time in prayer this week listening for the Holy Spirit. Keep a journal noting what you hear and sense. Throughout the day pray, "Come and fill my life, Holy Spirit" and write down your experiences at the end of each day.

PART FOUR:
At War with the Devil

For our struggle is not against flesh and blood, but
against the rulers, against the authorities, against the powers
of this dark world and against the spiritual forces of evil
in the heavenly realms.
(Ephesians 6:12 NIV)

14
Recognizing the Enemy

Everyone enjoys a good vacation. However, as we navigate this relational journey with our Father and King, it is important to understand we are not in the Kingdom simply to enjoy a beach-resort vacation. This side of eternity we are in an all-out war on the battlefield called life. While we have been brought into God's Kingdom and have nothing to fear with Jesus as our King, we still have a very real enemy. As mentioned in chapter one, the Bible refers to this enemy as *the satan*, meaning "the adversary" or "the accuser." Satan seeks to destroy our life with Christ and keep us from relationship with God as much as possible.

Many of us tend to think of the devil as an imaginary red figure with horns and a pointed tail, carrying a harmless pitchfork. But that's not the description the Bible gives. Satan is a literal being whom the Bible says is a thief whose intent is to "steal and kill and destroy" (John 10:10). The Apostle Peter warns us to be watchful and alert because "[our] enemy the devil prowls around like a roaring lion looking for someone to devour" (1 Peter 5:8). Woah. A lion? Someone to devour? That is some intense imagery! But Peter doesn't tell us this so we will be afraid; he tells us so we can be alert and aware.

As the name *Satan* indicates, the enemy's primary tactic is to deceive and accuse. Satan has no power in a believer's life except what is given to him through agreement. Satan can't force anyone to do anything; he can only suggest it. We see this at play from from the very beginning in the Garden of Eden. Satan came to Eve in the form of a serpent and suggested that God wasn't really who He said He was, that He wouldn't actually do what He said He would do. The serpent led her to believe the lie that God was holding out on her. Adam and Eve both took the bait and believed a lie over God's truth. They allowed Satan's lie to take root in their hearts and thus sin entered our domain.

Satan is still using this same basic tactic thousands of years later. He tries to persuade us to believe lies about God, about ourselves, about our circumstances, and about other people. Satan's primary goal is not to keep you from believing, but rather to get you to believe something that isn't true. Often these lies seem to have a grain of truth in them. Satan doesn't create new ideas, he simply twists the truth just enough to lead us astray. The Bible calls him "a liar and the father of lies" (John 8:44), and tells us he disguises himself as "an angel of light" (2 Corinthians 11:14). But we don't have to be misled. We know Satan is a deceiver and we can learn to discern between God's truth and Satan's false accusations. Second Corinthians 2:11 tells us we will not be outwitted by Satan, "for we are not unaware of his designs." The Apostle Paul, in his letter to the Ephesians, tells us how we can "stand firm against all strategies of the devil" by putting on spiritual "armor," one of the pieces being the belt of truth (6:10-18).

If you are in a battle it is crucial to understand who the real enemy is. But even then you don't focus your attention on what the enemy is doing; you tune your ear to the voice of your commander and listen for his direction. As we become aware of the enemy and his tactics, we keep our focus on Jesus and our ears open to His guidance and command. He will lead us into victory.

—Questions to Consider —

• List the pieces of spiritual armor we have been given, as seen in Ephesians 6:10-18. How does this armor help us in our fight against evil?

• What lies have you believed that need to be replaced with God's truth? *Ask God to reveal His truth to you for each lie.*

15
The Unseen Battleground

The battle for our souls is unlike any other battle we face here on earth. It does not involve M16s and grenade launchers or uppercuts and left hooks. This battle is actually invisible! The Apostle Paul tells us:

> We are not fighting against flesh-and-blood enemies, but against evil rulers and authorities of the unseen world, against mighty powers in this dark world, and against evil spirits in the heavenly places (Ephesians 6:12 NLT).

There are some days it is easy to feel that our boss or spouse or mother-in-law is the enemy, but the truth is the enemy is unseen. Our battle is not with people—it's against the forces of evil. If we are to win the war we must understand the nature of the battle. Otherwise, we will fight the wrong battle with the wrong weapons and find ourselves tired, frustrated, and losing.

So how do we fight what we cannot see? Jesus taught that what occurs in the visible (natural) realm has its beginning point in the invisible (spiritual) realm. (This principle can be seen in Jesus' Kingdom parables, specifically the parables of the mustard seed and leaven in Matthew 13:31-32.) This is true both of the Kingdom of Heaven and the forces of evil. Satan, the adversary, seeks to draw us away from life in the Kingdom through deceit and accusation primarily by waging war against our mind. Satan is not *in* our minds nor does he read our minds, but he is pretty good at making suggestions. These suggestions may come as temptations to sin, thoughts of shame and condemnation, accusations, or confusion. We fall prey to these landmines when we choose to accept them as truth and agree with them.

If we agree with the enemy's lies long enough, they become strongholds in our lives. A *stronghold* is a "fortress," a place surrounded by walls and meant to keep people out. In spiritual terms, a stronghold can refer to a mindset or pattern of thought that is built on false accusations or misunderstandings and holds us captive, keeping us from experiencing the life of joy and peace for which God created us. The Apostle Paul gives us some insight into the nature of strongholds in 2 Corinthians 10:3-5:

> For though we walk in the flesh, we are not waging war according to the flesh. For the weapons of our warfare are not of the flesh but have divine power to destroy strongholds. We destroy arguments and every lofty opinion raised against the knowledge of God, and take every thought captive to obey Christ.

Any pattern of thinking or logic that doesn't line up with God's truth becomes a barrier that is intended to keep us from the knowledge of God. If we are to follow Jesus fully and freely in this Kingdom journey, we must tear down all walls that have been built up to keep us from Jesus. We must also form correct beliefs based on the truth of God's character and His Word. We do this by recognizing and acknowledging each lie and "taking [them] captive to obey Christ." This means calling out the lie, realizing your authority over it, and declaring God's truth about your situation. You and I were never meant to live bound up and walled in. We are called to freedom! But we will be free only if we take the time to honestly acknowledge what may be keeping us from following Jesus and deal with it head on.

— Questions to Consider —

• In what areas have you allowed the enemy to build a stronghold, keeping you from knowing complete freedom? (What logic or way of thinking might you be practicing that doesn't line up with God's thoughts?)

• John 8:31-32 tells us if we abide in God's Word we will know the truth, and the truth will set us free. How might knowing the truth free us?

16
The Battle for Our Hearts, Part A

While much of the battle takes place in the mind, the reason for the battle is our heart. The *heart* is a reference to our inner person, the thoughts and feelings and beliefs from which we subconsciously operate. It guides everything we say and do. It is for this reason that at the heart of every spiritual battle is our heart.

King Solomon warned of the importance of keeping watch over our hearts: "Above all else, guard your heart, for everything you do flows from it" (Proverbs 4:23 NIV).

Like a poisonous root would poison the whole plant, issues of the heart affect every area of our lives—including (and especially) how we relate to God and people. Unforgiveness, hatred, jealousy, bitterness, and pride all begin in the unseen recesses of the heart. But what happens in the heart does not stay in the heart. Given time, these vices move into and take over every area of our lives and affect the way we think, what we say, and how we behave.

One of the most prominent heart issues that forms strongholds in our lives is unforgiveness. Unforgiveness is the result of a hurt or "offense" that leads to a real or perceived debt. Someone may have said something hurtful. Someone may have caused mental, physical, or emotional harm due to violence or neglect. Someone may have literally stolen something. Regardless, we feel someone owes us something (whether tangible or intangible) and we are not going to let them off the hook until they pay what they owe. This debt may be an apology, affection, money, or any number of things of which we like to keep track. The hurt is real, whether intended or not, and so the debt they owe is real to us. We want justice!

Or at least we think we want justice. The problem with unforgiveness is that it highlights the indebtedness of others and ignores the reality of our own indebtedness. We demand others pay for their sins but cry for mercy and grace for our own shortcomings and offenses. We want to receive forgiveness without having to pay it forward.

Unforgiveness is a sin for which we often feel justified, but Jesus gave many very serious warnings about the ramifications of unforgiveness. What we do with these real or perceived debts against us will determine the level of freedom we experience in our own lives. Jesus taught if we refuse to let go and release others from their debts, neither will He release us from our debts (Matthew 18:23-35). When we choose not to forgive, we lock ourselves in a spiritual prison. The only way to be released and walk in true freedom is to forgive those who have hurt us, releasing them from their indebtedness to us.

Forgiveness does not mean ignoring the reality of an offense. It doesn't mean hiding our feelings and pretending it was no big deal or that nothing ever happened. It simply means we no longer require payment from this person or expect them to in some way earn our pardon. They are free. So how do we forgive? It starts by going back to our place of hurt and receiving healing from the only true source of healing: Jesus. We must first be forgiven of our own faults and then find healing for our woundedness. As we let go of offense and are made whole, our hearts are freed to grow in health and walk in Christ's love, loving others as He loves us, no matter what.

— Questions to Consider —

• Is there anyone that you feel owes you because of a wrong done to you? What can you do to make things right? (See Matthew 18:15-20.)

• The Bible says our life with God is directly affected by our love for people (John 15:9-12). How does unforgiveness toward another person affect our relationship with God?

17
The Battle for Our Hearts, Part B

The danger of being offended is not the only reason for guarding our hearts. The *heart* also speaks of desire. It is the treasure trove of our deepest longings. That's why God is after our heart. He doesn't want routine religion and memorized rituals—He wants a real relationship grounded in loyalty and desire. The enemy works overtime to keep us preoccupied with lesser substitutes of relationship. We call these lesser substitutes "idols."

You may have thought idolatry was a title reserved for worshiping wooden images or golden calves, but we commit idolatry any time we place someone or something at the center of our hearts, where Jesus rightfully belongs. It is here in our hearts where we assign worth to people, places, and things. While we tend to think of church songs and religious services or pagan rituals and weird sacrifices when we hear the word *worship*, worship really refers to anything to which our heart assigns worth. It speaks of what we value. To worship a person, place, or thing is to give it our heart's attention. And while we have the tendency to give our attention to many things, our hearts were created to worship God and God alone.

God is not against our desires. He is actually for them. But our desires are only satisfied fully in one place: God's presence. Outside of His presence our desires are disordered and will cause confusion and heartache. Only when our hearts are wholly given to God and we find satisfaction in Him, will our love for other things be in order.

If we're not guarding our hearts, things other than God—even good things—become objects of worship. We may worship our pursuit of power and success, pleasure, hopes of fame and fortune, or something as innocent as the desire to get married, have a family, and live a good, comfortable life. None of these are inherently wrong. The problem is when we pursue the gift instead of the Giver, what was created instead of the One who created. Soon enough, these harmless substitutes creep in and steal our attention and affection away from God.

This is what makes idolatry so dangerous. It attacks our relationship with God by dividing our heart. Just as we would grow jealous over and never tolerate a casual side fling for the one we deeply love, God does not want to share us with other pursuits and passions. He is a jealous God in the sense that He wants us solely for Himself (see Exodus 20:5; 34:14; Deuteronomy 4:24). He has created us to be a people belonging to Him. He wants to be the desire of our hearts, the pursuit of our lives, and the focus of all our love and worship.

Our response to idols is not simply to remove them but to replace them. The only way to find true satisfaction for our souls is to move our attention away from false gods and to shift our focus back to our Creator. A God-centered life is not "God first," then everything else. It is God—period—and everything we desire is found in Him. In God's love we are enabled to love everything else rightly. But apart from God's love, even good things become deadly things. We must remove the idols and invite Jesus to fill every space of our hearts. As long as our hearts remain wholly His, the enemy doesn't stand a chance in this battle.

– Questions to Consider –

• In this season of life, what is your heart's greatest desire?

• How might disordered desires cause chaos and anxiety in our lives?

18
Breaking Free & Moving Forward

None of us are perfect. We have all sinned. We have all betrayed our Father and wound up as prisoners of war. We have all failed (Romans 3:23). But failure isn't final—and sin doesn't have to have the last word. When we find that we have been living in response to a lie—whether that be evidenced in a secret sin of the heart or blatant rebellion against God—the only way to make things right is to stop and admit our need for help, and turn away from sin and back to God. In Biblical terms, we must confess, repent, and believe.

Confession means to speak up and admit that not everything is okay. It means owning up to our faults. Admitting we are in the wrong can be terrifying, but it is a necessary first step to freedom. Tell God what you've done. Tell Him what is in your heart and on your mind. Confess your sin to the One who can save you. The Bible teaches that as we confess to God, we are forgiven; and as we confess to fellow believers, we are healed (1 John 1:9; James 5:16).

Once we've talked to God openly about our hurt, habit, or hang-up, we need to break agreement with sin. If we've been living as a prisoner to sin, it's because we've been agreeing with it! We must renounce sin and part ways with it. To *renounce* means to declare the end of one's claim, right, or possession of something—to "refuse to recognize or abide by any longer; to declare that one will no longer engage in or support" (*Merriam-Webster*

Dictionary). Essentially, we are ending our partnership with this wrong thought/relationship/activity and transferring our alliance and allegiance elsewhere. The Biblical word for this is *repentance*. It means to "change one's mind about something" or to "change directions." To repent of sin is to confess it, change the way we think about it, and to subsequently change our behavior.

Finally, it's so important after we have confessed and repented of sin to actually return to God. Ask God to change your mind but also to change your heart. Don't stay stuck after you've been made free! Realize that it's possible to confess sin, sincerely try to part ways with it, but remain depressed and defeated. Once we've poured our hearts out to God in confession and repentance, we must receive His forgiveness and allow Him to bring us into alignment with His heart. Spend time listening for God and believe you have been forgiven. Trust that He has restored you to right relationship with Himself. We are not ugly ducklings or second-rate in His eyes. He calls us His sons and daughters.

This final step of turning to God and believing He is for us is an act of faith. We won't always *feel* forgiven. It's not always easy to see ourselves the way God sees us. But in doing so, we trust God's Word above our feelings and place Him as the final authority of our lives. We choose to walk by faith and not by sight, believing His gracious and merciful ways are better than ours (2 Corinthians 5:7; Isaiah 55:6-9). We replace the enemy's lies with God's truth that we are fully forgiven and free from condemning accusations. We are cleansed, accepted and chosen, more than conquerors, heirs to the Kingdom, and beloved children (1 John 1:9; Romans 8:1, 14-17, 37). No shame. No guilt. We believe Jesus' sacrificial death has paid for our sin and has made a way for us to be in right relationship with our Father. We picture His smiling face, feel His sense of approval and loving embrace, and live in complete freedom. (See the "Prayer" following the "Conclusion" of this book for an in-depth model prayer.)

Though we are in a war, God has not left us helpless or hopeless. He never calls us to a battle He does not intend for us to win. He is with us and has given us everything we need not only to face this battle but to endure it and emerge victorious. In the next section, we will look at some ways to be strengthened in relationship with God despite facing opposition from a very real enemy.

– Questions to Consider –

• What do you need to confess and repent of in order to receive forgiveness and walk in freedom?

• What truth do you need to believe about you or your situation so you can think and live more like Jesus?

– Application Exercise –
Sharing Your Struggle

Get together with a friend and share some of your struggles. Ask this friend to pray with you about what you are facing. You may also consider asking a local church if they have a prayer ministry that focuses on deliverance and inner healing.

See the "Recommended Resources" appendix at the back of this book for links to model prayers that will help you overcome and walk in freedom.

PART FIVE:
Training To Win

*Every athlete in training submits to strict discipline. . . . I run
straight for the finish line; that is why I am like a boxer who
does not waste his punches. I harden my body with blows
and bring it under complete control, to keep myself from
being disqualified after having called others to the contest.*
(1 Corinthians 9:25-27 GNT)

19
The Necessity of Discipline

"The more you sweat in training, the less you bleed in war." This saying, attributed to the U.S. Navy Seals, reminds us of the seriousness and importance of practice and preparation. If you've ever embarked on a New Year's resolution to eat less and workout more or made the decision to run several miles a day in preparation for a marathon, you know training is difficult. Any time we get serious about getting in shape and living healthy, it doesn't take long to realize it requires a lot of sacrifice and self-discipline. To achieve a goal we have to manage our appetites and change some habits. Skip the brownie. Get up earlier or go to bed later. Push through to the last set. Training is hard work!

As we continue on this journey to know Jesus and make Him known, we realize living like Jesus is not a walk in the park. We already acknowledged we are living in a spiritual war zone. In letters to his spiritual son, Timothy, the Apostle Paul says to "fight the good fight of faith" and encourages Timothy to endure suffering "as a good soldier of Christ Jesus" (1 Timothy 6:12; 2 Timothy 2:3-4). Being a good soldier is no easy task. It requires sacrifice, commitment, and discipline. It necessitates preparation and training. Soldiers don't wait until the enemy is at their doorstep with a grenade in hand to train for battle. They daily discipline their minds and bodies so as to be ready for combat. So it is on our journey with Christ. We must train. We must discipline ourselves, body, soul, and spirit.

Paul also advised Timothy, "Train yourself for godliness" (1 Timothy 4:7). In effect, he said, "Don't just work out to get a buff body here on earth—train your inner man and be strengthened to live like Jesus in this life and the one to come." Ask anyone who has disciplined themselves through training how or why they do it, and we would most likely hear them say something about the end goal—the results. The way to go hard and push through when the pain comes is by keeping the endgame in mind.

While an obvious reward of discipline is getting better, stronger, and more fit to fight and win, there's more to it than that. Discipline comes into play in relationship as well. Sometimes we must fight for relationship. There are times love is a good feeling and comes naturally; and there are other times we don't feel a thing and must choose a loving response simply because we are committed to the relationship. It is in these times of doing what is right even when it is hard that we truly grow. Not only do we grow as a person, we grow deeper in relationship. This is the true reward of discipline. Staying the course when the journey is difficult, submitting to one another when it doesn't seem to make sense and brings discomfort, and loving when we aren't feeling it at all brings us to a greater place of depth and intimacy in relationship.

This is why we train. This is why we fight. The reward of relationship with our God is at stake. Dethroning self and dying to old desires is difficult, and the opposition is real, but if we will press on through the pain of discipline we will come to know the joy of relationship.

– Questions to Consider –

• How does discipline help to achieve a goal?

• How might discipline help you to follow Jesus?

20
Working the Plan

Two ways to help ensure success when training is to follow a plan and to work with a trainer. Simply put, if we're not sure what to do we probably won't do it. And sometimes, even when we know what to do, we need someone to help motivate us to do it. God has given us both a plan and a trainer in the Holy Spirit. He is our faithful guide. Just as Jesus said, the Holy Spirit "will teach you all things and will remind you of everything" Jesus has taught (John 14:26). The Holy Spirit is the one who shows us what to do and gives us courage and the ability to do it.

If you remember the pattern of relationship from several chapters ago (*revelation > response > relationship*), working the plan would be the "repeat" portion of the cycle. Without discipline and endurance, we will at some point come up short of passion and progress and quit running for the prize. The old maxim proves true, "Life is a marathon, not a sprint." You don't run a marathon without training. And you don't train in a day. Training is the practice and result of repeated exercises. Over. And over. And over again. Day after day after day. The Apostle Paul reminds us again why this training is important:

> Don't you realize that in a race everyone runs, but only one person gets the prize? So run to win! All athletes are disciplined in their training. They do it to win a prize that will fade away, but we

do it for an eternal prize. So I run with purpose in every step. I am not just shadowboxing. I discipline my body like an athlete, training it to do what it should. Otherwise, I fear that after preaching to others I myself might be disqualified (1 Corinthians 9:24-27).

While athletes discipline themselves to win a trophy that will eventually lose its shine, we discipline ourselves for a relationship and rewards that last forever! This is why the Bible encourages us to set our eyes on Jesus, get rid of anything that would distract us, and run with patient endurance (Hebrews 12:1-2). Follow the trainer. Work the plan.

The plan, of course, is to obey what Jesus has said. If we were to boil His commands down to two, they would be *love God* and *love people*. This is the plan. Ultimately, only the work of the Holy Spirit and a relationship with Jesus can enable us to carry out this plan successfully. But there are practices that serve as spiritual stretching and strengthening exercises that aid us in keeping our hearts soft and our lives focused as we seek to follow Jesus. These practices are holy habits that have been repeated by friends of Jesus through the centuries and have come to be called "spiritual disciplines." These disciplines help build up spiritual muscle and the stamina required for a life of joyful obedience over the long haul.

What we must keep in mind as we practice these disciplines is that they are merely tools. They are not the prize, nor are they the reason for the prize. Done wrongly, exercises can actually harm rather than help an athlete. That is why we always submit to the Holy Spirit. He will show us how to use these disciplines to experience an ever-deepening relationship with God and keep us from falling into stale religion and deadly self-reliance. With this in mind, let's take a look at these holy habits. We will divide them into two categories—disciplines of abstinence and disciplines of engagement—and do a brief overview of each in the coming chapters.

– Questions to Consider –

• Give an example of a time you attempted to do something that required sacrifice, commitment, and discipline. How did it go? What made it successful or unsuccessful?

• In what areas of life do you need the Holy Spirit to help you practice discipline?

21
Disciplines of Abstinence

Disciplines of abstinence are those practices which require drawing away from or choosing to go without for a period of time in order to draw closer to God. To be of benefit these practices should be paired with disciplines of engagement (to be discussed in the next two chapters). We abstain from one thing so as to engage more fully in another.

Silence & Solitude

Silence comes easier for some than others, but it's important for us all to take the time to slow down, stop the chatterbox, and just be with God. Silence is a discipline in halting the voices within and around us in an effort to intentionally listen. We take time to stop speaking and simply listen for God's voice in the silence. It is often in these times that we hear most clearly.

Silence is often by necessity accompanied by solitude. Solitude is intentionally taking time to step away from the crowds and be alone with Jesus. The Bible tells of several times when Jesus would draw away from people and spend time alone with Father God (Matthew 14:23; Mark 1:35; Luke 5:16; 6:12). In these times Jesus received encouragement and direction to continue doing the work He was sent to do. Practicing solitude in our fast-paced world requires being intentional in creating time and space away. It might even mean getting a calendar out and proactively scheduling times to get away just to be with God.

Sabbath

Sabbath rest is a critical component of the Christian life. The word *sabbath* comes from a Hebrew word that means to "stop," "cease," or "keep." The general idea is to step away from the daily grind of life and rest. God set an example for us at creation. He made the universe and all that is within it in six days, and then on the seventh day He rested. He knew we would need His example to learn this discipline of rest. Biblical sabbath means setting aside one day each week to pause our work and the constant striving to accomplish and allow our body, soul, and spirit time to be refreshed. No worrying, no stress; just rest and worship. God is able to do more in our time of obedient rest than we could do through our own frantic and exhausting efforts to achieve and succeed. Put simply, practicing sabbath is an exercise of trust.

Fasting

Fasting is a discipline mentioned several times in Scripture that involves abstaining from food (and in special cases, water) for a time of increased spiritual devotion. When we fast, we are practicing self-control and placing our spirit in its rightful place ahead of our body. Denying our natural desires can help us say "yes" to God's desires rather than following what feels good to our flesh. The goal behind fasting is not to starve ourselves but to discipline our body so our spirit can take the lead and help us to focus on God. Fasting should be practiced with caution for those with medical conditions as it is directly correlated to our physical health.

– Questions to Consider –

• How can withdrawing from one thing help us to more fully engage in another?

• Have you ever practiced any of these disciplines? What were the results?

22
Disciplines of Engagement, Part A

Disciplines of engagement are practices that call for active participation. Rather than drawing away from something, we interact with God by doing something. These are most helpful when practiced on a daily basis as a natural rhythm of life.

Scripture Reading & Meditation

Even if reading is not your favorite activity, it is essential to make reading the Bible a regular part of your life as you seek to know God in a deeper way. Romans 10:17 says, "Faith comes from hearing, and hearing from the word of Christ." When we listen to and read Scripture we are filled with faith and can then respond to Christ's words in obedience and experience growth. Reading the Bible is the primary way to find out who God is, what He is like, and what His will is.

Meditation, best practiced alongside silence and solitude, may sound like a strange mystical practice reserved for new-agers and monks of Eastern religions, but that's not what we're talking about here. It's really very simple. Meditation is intentional thinking. In our relationship with God it is helpful to take time regularly to stop and ponder the things of God. You may read a Scripture verse over and over, thinking and praying about what God is saying. You may call to mind something specific God has spoken to you in the past. Or you may think about the goodness of God or another of His qualities. As we think, so we become. As we meditate on God's words, His thoughts become our thoughts and our lives are transformed to become more like Jesus.

Prayer & Reflection

The practice of prayer is the discipline of conversation. Prayer is not merely wishing upon a star—it is listening to and speaking with the God of the universe! Spending daily time in communication with God is how we come to know Him, grow in love with Him, and learn of His desires. In prayer we also share our lives with Him. We tell Him of our joys, our pains, and our sorrows. A great way to practice this is by journaling. Reflect on what God has said or is saying and write it down. Take note of how you are feeling and write a letter to God about it. Make a list of the promises God has made to you and spend time meditating on those promises. Tell God how you feel! Just as communication is key to building and sustaining any relationship, so it is in friendship with God.

Community

As the saying goes, "No man is an island." This is especially true of a Christ follower. Though it is important to withdraw and practice seasons of silence and solitude, the true Christian life is one lived in community. Hebrews 10:24-25 tells us to continually gather together with other believers to encourage one another and to motivate one another to excel in love and in doing good deeds. Enjoying community doesn't require being an extrovert, but it does mean being intentional. Practicing community is an important skill to develop in living a godly life! We must prioritize consistent and quality time together with other believers whether in church gatherings, discussion groups, or meeting in one another's houses to remain healthy and continue deepening our faith in Jesus.

— Questions to Consider —

• How might meditating on Scripture change the way you think and behave? How can you implement Scripture reading and meditation in your daily routine this week?

• How can Scripture reading and prayer be joined with the discipline of community?

23
Disciplines of Engagement, Part B

Many of the things Jesus taught were countercultural and even somewhat counterintuitive. His teaching on giving is one of those things. We tend to want to get all we can, can all we get, and sit on the lid (or something like that). But Christ calls us to live radical lives of service and giving where we live for more than ourselves. The following disciplines require getting our eyes off of self and caring for those around us.

Giving

Giving doesn't come naturally. Actually, it takes a transformed heart and a lot of practice! In giving, we deny the tendency for self-centeredness and instead enrich the lives of others. The Bible teaches that giving is really a practice in sowing. What we give is a seed. As we give, our seed is sown and in turn it multiplies and produces more than it would have if left in our hands.

While we usually relate generosity to money, there are other ways to give. One such way is service. While most of the world sends the message that life is all about ME, ME, ME, and you should "have it your way"—Jesus says otherwise. The world's path to success is to climb the "ladder," but Jesus taught His disciples that anyone who wants to be great should humble himself and serve (Mark 9:35). By practicing service, we regularly remind ourselves that life is not all about me but about others.

Worship

We tend to think of church music or special services when we hear the word *worship*, but true worship is something we practice every day. Worship is assigning worth to something. When we clap our hands for a talented artist or say "thank you" to the cook for an excellent meal, we are praising that individual. The way we worship God is not just through clapping and singing but in the way we do life. Romans 12:1 tells us offering our lives wholly to God is true worship. Anything we give God from our hearts can be worship. Sending a letter to a friend, setting the table for dinner, saying "Thank You" to God for all He has done, journaling all the ways the world amazes us, are all wonderful ways to worship God. Whether we are eating, writing, creating, or sharing, we can "do all to the glory of God" (1 Corinthians 10:31).

Celebration

Along with worship, an important but not-too-often considered practice is that of celebration. In the Old Testament, God actually commanded the nation of Israel to throw parties! They had several feasts each year where they were commanded to eat, drink, and celebrate. They were not to mourn on those days. They were not to go about moping. They were to practice the discipline of celebration. Too often, Christians become known as solemn and cynical individuals. It doesn't have to be this way—we have reason to be the happiest people alive!

One way to practice being happy is to be thankful. As we realize all that God has blessed us with, celebration comes more naturally. When we think of who He is and what He is done, we realize there is always reason to celebrate.

As we practice these disciplines, it is important to remember the goal is relationship. It will always be about relationship. We don't want to fall into the trap of trying to use these practices as a way to validate ourselves before God. We are validated by Jesus' grace. We simply use these practices as a way to stay spiritually fit so we can run well and receive the prize of knowing Him!

– Questions to Consider –

• How do generosity, worship, and celebration help us to get our eyes off of self?

• How might these disciplines enhance your relationship with God?

– Application Exercise –
Practicing Holy Habits

Commit to practicing one or more of the disciplines of abstinence this week in addition to your regular disciplines of engagement. You may also want to set aside some time to research and study other spiritual disciplines. These could include confession, submission, study, chastity, and secrecy (Matthew 6:1-18), among others. Share your thoughts on your experience with a friend or coach.

PART SIX:
Gifts & Graces

*As each one has received a special gift, employ it in serving
one another as good stewards of the manifold grace of God.*
(1 Peter 4:10 NASB)

24
Living on Mission

God, in His wisdom, does nothing without purpose. While Jesus was on earth, He walked alongside of and taught His disciples. He gave them authority to heal the sick, raise the dead, restore the outcast, and cast out demons (Matthew 10:8). Following Christ's death and resurrection, the Holy Spirit was sent to continue walking with and teaching all who follow Christ. Acts 1:8 declares that those who waited for the Holy Spirit would receive power. Power for what? The verse continues, "You will be my witnesses in Jerusalem and in all Judea and Samaria, and to the end of the earth." The Holy Spirit gives us power to be witnesses for Christ to the world!

We have boldness and authority to testify to His life, death, and resurrection. We are filled with the Spirit because God wants to live in us. We bear the fruit of the Spirit because God wants to make us like Himself. We are empowered by the Spirit so we can accomplish God's mission of making disciples throughout the entire world. The Holy Spirit's aim is to exalt Jesus and make Him famous, and He wants us to partner with Him to ensure this happen.

This sounds like a big task . . . and it is! But God isn't asking us to do this empty-handed. Through the Holy Spirit, God has given us all we need to accomplish His grand purpose of bringing His Kingdom to our world. One of the ways the Holy Spirit equips us is by giving a variety of tools to help us along the way. Romans 12:6 tells us, "In his grace, God has given us different gifts for doing certain things well." These "gifts" are special skills, abilities, and people that point the world to Jesus and strengthen His Church. Another way to think of these gifts is as "enabling graces." They are the result of God's grace upon our lives and enable us to effectively communicate God's grace to those in our church community and to the world. How cool is that? God has shown us His kindness and then equipped us to share His kindness with those around us—both those in the Kingdom and those yet to participate in His reign.

As we look at these gifts of grace, it's important to understand that while fruit is grown, gifts are given. Neither is earned. The fruit of the Spirit (love, joy, peace, etc.) is developed over time as a result of living in relationship with the Holy Spirit. Gifts, on the other hand are abilities that God sovereignly chooses to give to us (see 1 Corinthians 12). Gifts are given in a moment and developed over time but they always remain gifts. They are not a sign of maturity. Love is a sign of relationship and maturity; gifts are evidence of God's kindness and attentive care.

In the next three chapters, we will look at some of these enabling graces and see how they help make Jesus famous.

– Questions to Consider –

• What is the difference between the fruit of the Spirit and gifts of the Spirit?

• How are spiritual gifts evidence of God's grace?

25
Revealing God's Power

There are many gifts God gives, but we will first explore the gifts mentioned in 1 Corinthians 12. Here, the Apostle Paul references a variety of abilities the Holy Spirit inspires and enables. Paul calls them "manifestations" of the Spirit. This simply means they manifest or reveal something or, in this case, Someone. While each gift is unique, they all are given by the same Holy Spirit and support the same objective of pointing people to Jesus. Let's take a brief look at a definition and example of each one.

Word of wisdom: When a person receives divine counsel or instruction (whether for themselves or for someone else) as to what to do in a given situation (see 1 Kings 3:16-28; Acts 17:16-23). God may use you to advise a close friend in a specific course of action regarding the business they recently purchased or a relationship they began.

Word of knowledge: When a person is given divine knowledge about something they otherwise could not have known (see John 4:16-19; Acts 5:1-11). Suppose while speaking with a young person, you have a confident, unprompted sense that he has been feeling a pull towards a vocation in the arts—something of which you previously had no knowledge—and, upon sharing, you learn that this is exactly what he has been feeling.

Faith: When a person has a confident assurance that God will do something (see Mark 4:35-40; Acts 14:8-10).

Imagine God has told you to purchase a building that cost one million dollars and you have no idea how that could be possible. When the Holy Spirit has given you the gift of faith you will not only believe the impossible is possible, but to be expected!

Healing: When a person is used by God to restore someone to full health (see Luke 9:1, 6; Acts 28:8-9). This could happen through a word spoken or a simple touch. You pray for Ashley, who is asthmatic, and her lungs are restored to perfect health and she throws her inhaler away, no longer needing it (true story!).

Miracles: When a person is given power to do something naturally impossible (see Matthew 14:13-21; Acts 19:11-12). Suppose you pray for a rainstorm to stop and it does, or for a man to be raised from the dead and he is—that's miraculous!

Prophecy: When a person speaks on behalf of God, revealing His thoughts about a person or situation (see Matthew 16:17-18; Acts 11:27-28). God may speak to you about an event that is going to happen in the future, or He may simply nudge you to speak with your neighbor to remind her that she is loved.

Discerning of spirits: When a person is able to perceive what is guiding someone else's motives: whether good or evil (see Matthew 9:2-4; Acts 13:6-11). Imagine three people were interested in the same role within your organization. After talking it over with God, He reveals to you that one has issues with anger and another refuses to submit to authority, enabling you to make a wise and healthy decision.

Tongues: When a person is supernaturally enabled to speak in a language not his own, whether earthly or heavenly (see Acts 2:1-12; 10:44-48). Suppose you are in a foreign city and begin praying in a language unknown to you. Suddenly, the girl next to you, who is Taiwanese, reveals she can understand what you are saying because you are speaking her mother tongue!

Interpretation of tongues: When a person is supernaturally enabled to translate words spoken in a language not their own, whether earthly or heavenly (see 1 Corinthians 14:1-13, 26-28). You hear someone give a word for the church in an unfamiliar language but sense God is giving you words to say, so you speak them out. Later you discover that what you said in your language matched what was said in the other language.

These gifts are diverse in nature but all come from the same Holy Spirit. How creative God is! Next, we will look at gifts given by Jesus to His Church.

– Questions to Consider –

• How have you encountered God through one or more of these gifts? How did the gift(s) bring glory to God?

• What do these gifts reveal to us about God?

26
Jesus' Gifts to the Church

Whereas the gifts mentioned in 1 Corinthians are graces given by the Holy Spirit, the Book of Ephesians reveals five gifts given *by Jesus* for the benefit of His Church.

> And [Jesus] gave the apostles, the prophets, the evangelists, the shepherds and teachers, to equip the saints for the work of ministry, for building up the body of Christ, until we all attain to the unity of the faith and of the knowledge of the Son of God, to mature manhood, to the measure of the stature of the fullness of Christ (4:11-13).

While the gifts listed in 1 Corinthians 12 are abilities, the gifts here are actually people! Jesus has given His Church these specific types of people who, when operating in their giftings, will help the Church grow to be healthy and mature and be more like Himself. Their role is to equip believers to serve one another and the world, bringing people together to know and trust Christ. Let's take a look at each of these gifts.

Apostles are God's entrepreneurs and overseers in the Kingdom. The word *apostle* means "sent one." Apostles are sent by God to initiate and oversee Kingdom ventures. It is important to realize there were only 12 founding apostles of the Church. That will not change. Apostles in our time are those whom God calls to preach the Gospel, start churches where there are none, and parent these churches into health and growth.

Prophets are those who speak for God and remind the Church of what God is saying and how to follow Him faithfully in changing times. This is different than just operating in the gift of prophecy. A prophet's role is to help guide a congregation and keep it in line with God's heart and vision. The prophet calls us back to the Word of God in every season.

Evangelists are especially gifted in sharing the message of the Gospel and introducing people to relationship with Jesus. They love telling the good news of Jesus where it has never been heard before. Evangelists help keep the church focused on its mission to make disciples in every place at all times.

Pastors are like shepherds. They come alongside of and oversee a community of people, caring for them and helping them to follow Jesus fully. They are gifted to lead and administer, ensuring that the congregation grows together and none are left behind.

Teachers are those who are gifted in explaining God's words and God's ways so people can clearly understand. Alongside the pastor, teachers help guard God's people from straying into false teaching and unimportant debates. The roles of pastor and teacher often go hand-in-hand.

An easy way to remember these roles (often called the "five-fold giftings") is to use the hand as a memory aid. The apostle is represented by the thumb as it works with each of the other fingers to grip and function properly. The forefinger is the prophet as it is used to point the way or to confront and correct as needed. The middle finger is the farthest-reaching finger, so it helps us to remember the role of the evangelist. The pastor is remembered by the ring finger. This speaks of covenant and commitment, indicative of the relationship between the pastor and those he leads. Finally, the pinky reminds us of the teacher as the pinky balances and strengthens the hand.

Each of these roles are incredible gifts Jesus gives to help His Church grow to its full potential and enable it to minister effectively. Thank God for these people!

– Questions to Consider –

• How are these roles functioning in your local expression of Christ's Church?

• How might these gifts strengthen a congregation?

27
Uniquely Gifted to Serve

The final place we will look to learn of these gifts of grace is Romans 12. Here, Paul reminds us that while God has given each of us different skills and abilities, we are still one body in Christ. Remembering this enables us to appreciate those differences rather than getting frustrated or growing jealous of others. When we have a proper understanding of our own giftings and how they relate to the bigger picture, we're more likely to use our giftings and to excel in them.

> For as in one body we have many members, and the members do not all have the same function, so we, though many, are one body in Christ, and individually members one of another. Having gifts that differ according to the grace given to us, let us use them: if prophecy, in proportion to our faith; if service, in our serving; the one who teaches, in his teaching; the one who exhorts, in his exhortation; the one who contributes, in generosity; the one who leads, with zeal; the one who does acts of mercy, with cheerfulness (vv. 4-8).

As we are learning to journey with Jesus in the Kingdom, it's important to discover how God has graced each of us differently. This frees us up to be the unique, custom masterpieces God made us to be. Then we can step into our particular gifting and use it skillfully rather than falling for the deadly trap of comparison, where we simply try to measure up to those around us. If you have the ability to sing, then sing! Are you especially crafty? Then create! Perhaps you'll see in yourself one of the gifts Paul mentions in Romans. Let's take a quick look at each of them.

Prophecy, also mentioned in 1 Corinthians 12, is to speak as God's representative. This may take the form of correction, a message of comfort, a revelation of something to come, or divine direction. In Romans 12, Paul tells us we should prophesy according to our measure of faith (how much are we willing to believe God for?).

Service literally means "to wait tables." This means being ready and willing to help out wherever needed. While this person may not be in the spotlight, they are eager to help others to advance the Kingdom.

Teaching is to "instruct" or "explain." Someone with a teaching gift can break down complicated truths and relate them to others in an understandable way.

Exhortation means to "encourage" and "strengthen." To exhort is to remind others of who God is, what He has done, and who we are as a result.

Giving refers to sincere and generous giving. Someone who operates in this gift finds true joy in helping others by giving what they have. It is no burden. Paul encourages those who walk in this gift to give generously. Don't hold back!

Leadership is the ability to lead the way, to assist others, and to protect and care for community. Those who help others by leading are to do so selflessly and with passion.

Acts of mercy speaks of help offered patiently and with compassion to those who are troubled or suffering. Those who are skilled in showing mercy should do so with a smile.

---

[2] It is important to note that the gift of prophecy does not carry the same weight as Biblical prophecy. While Scripture is absolute Truth and is authoritative, the gift of prophecy is subject to human error. Always compare a prophetic word with the words of God spoken through the Bible.

It is helpful to understand that Paul's writings aren't meant to form a complete inventory of spiritual gifts. They do, however, give us insight into the variety of ways God has enabled us to reveal His grace. How amazing that God would entrust us with the ability to reveal His grace! Understanding this awesome privilege, Paul encourages each of us to use our abilities according to the unique way God has gifted us.

– Questions to Consider –

• How does knowing all followers of Jesus form one body help us to appreciate others' differences?

• Give an example of a time you observed one of these gifts in action. How was God's grace (kindness, favor) made evident in it?

28
Learning to Love Well

Throughout his writings, Paul uses the image of a body to refer to how participants of Christ's Church relate to one another:

> The human body has many parts, but the many parts make up one whole body. So it is with the body of Christ (1 Corinthians 12:12 NLT).

It's common in Western culture to think of ourselves as isolated individuals, responsible solely for self, but this simply isn't true. When we surrender our lives to the King we become citizens of the Kingdom and are formed into a collective body. We are no longer our own but are actually "members one of another" (Romans 12:5). This may cause us to shudder a bit when we consider who we go to church with, but in Christ's eyes it is a beautiful thing.

God builds His Church with unique but interdependent pieces so we might learn to love well. There's the old saying, "You can choose your friends but you can't choose your family." The same could be said of the body of Christ. We don't get to pick and choose who should be a part of God's family or who we will be called to love and serve. We are one body. We also don't get to choose what part we are to play in the body. The arm can't change its function because it wants to be a leg. Neither can the pinky toe decide it wants to be the pointer finger for the day. Each part serves according to its design and for the good of the whole body. So it is with the body of Christ. Each person has been uniquely gifted by God to serve in a particular role that, when fulfilled, benefits everyone around them.

We must always remember people are greater than gifts. It may be tempting to think working a miracle or speaking a heavenly language is the ultimate mark of spirituality or Christian maturity, but the Bible teaches that the greatest gift of all is love (1 Corinthians 13:13).

> If I could speak all the languages of earth and of angels, but didn't love others, I would only be a noisy gong or a clanging cymbal. If I had the gift of prophecy, and if I understood all of God's secret plans and possessed all knowledge, and if I had such faith that I could move mountains, but didn't love others, I would be nothing. If I gave everything I have to the poor and even sacrificed my body, I could boast about it; but if I didn't love others, I would have gained nothing (1 Corinthians 13:1-3 NLT).

It is helpful to know this passage was written in the context of instructions on spiritual gifts and how the Church functions properly. The goal of operating in a spiritual gift is to love well. When we speak a word of prophesy to someone it isn't to show everyone how awesome we are—it is to reveal God's heart for that person and to love them as Jesus loves them. When we give generously, we aren't trying to earn a humanitarian award or add a point to our charity scorecard; we are learning to love. We are following God's example of giving to the world by giving of ourselves. John 3:16 begins, "For God so loved the world that He gave." This is the purpose of these remarkable skills and abilities. They are to reveal God's grace and be a channel by which we love people.

When we adopt this mindset and make loving people our goal, everyone wins. One person's gift brings encouragement to the whole church. Each part builds up and strengthens the whole. When the foot walks, the hand holds, and the eyes see, not only does the body function healthily, but God is glorified:

> As each has received a gift, use it to serve one another, as good stewards of God's varied grace: whoever speaks, as one who speaks oracles of God; whoever serves, as one who serves by the strength that God supplies—in order that in everything God may be glorified through Jesus Christ. To him belong glory and dominion forever and ever. Amen (1 Peter 4:10-11).

– Questions to Consider –

• What is the purpose of spiritual gifts?

• Give an example of how someone might be encouraged through a spiritual gift.

– Application Exercise –
Surveying Gifts

Complete a spiritual gifts assessment. Review the results with your coach. (Two free assessments can be found online at *spiritualgiftstest.com* and *giftstest.com*).

Spiritual Gifts

Romans 12:3-8	1 Corinthians 12:8-10	1 Corinthians 12:28-30	Ephesians 4:11
Prophecy	Words of Wisdom	Apostles	Apostles
Service	Words of Knowledge	Prophets	Prophets
Teaching	Faith	Teachers	Evangelists
Exhortation	Healing	Healing	Pastors
Giving	Miracles	Miracles	Teachers
Leadership	Prophecy	Administration	
Acts of Mercy	Discerning of Spirits	Helps	
	Tongues	Tongues	
	Interpretation of Tongues		

PART SEVEN:
On Mission with God

"But you shall receive power when the Holy Spirit has come upon you; and you shall be witnesses to Me in Jerusalem, and in all Judea and Samaria, and to the end of the earth."
(Acts 1:8 NKJV)

29
God's Glory, My Mission

Why are we here? What is the reason for our existence? Is there a point to this life? Some of the most important questions we ask have to do with purpose. A church document drafted in the mid-1600s cites man's greatest purpose as "to glorify God and enjoy Him forever."[3] Pastor and theologian John Piper has suggested, "Man's chief end is to glorify God *by* enjoying Him forever" (*Desiring God*).

We glorify God simply by being with Him and enjoying Him. This proves to be difficult for many of us. Rather than living as human *beings*, we often settle for life as human *doings*. We think we are here just to eat, sleep, work, and play, as if our purpose were to *find something to do and stay really busy at it*. But the first and primary way to bring God glory is to simply enjoy relationship with Him. Be with Him, be loved by Him, and give yourself freely and wholly to His care (John 15:1-11).

As we learn to first be with God, we can then join Him in bringing His Kingdom on earth as it is in Heaven. The Bible teaches of a day when God's glory will be known on earth to the same extent that "the waters cover the sea" (Habakkuk 2:14; Isaiah 11:9; Psalm 72:19; Numbers 14:21). Since the sea is made of one hundred percent water, we can anticipate that God's glory will be known everywhere

[3] Recorded in the *Westminster Catechism*, a document written in 1647 by English and Scottish theologians summarizing their teachings on various doctrines.

by everyone! Why is this important? Because when we experience God's glory we are changed. We recognize God as the brilliant, mighty Creator He is and ourselves as the small, finite creation we are (1 John 3:2). This awareness of God's glory brings everything into perspective and makes it all the more amazing that God would choose relationship with us!

God's mission all along has been to restore all people to relationship with Himself. He wants everyone everywhere to experience His glory: His goodness, His majesty, His power and grace. "For God so loved the world, that he gave his only Son, that whoever believes in him should not perish but have eternal life" (John 3:16). Jesus brings deeper insight into the meaning of "eternal life" when He says, "This is eternal life, that they know you, the only true God, and Jesus Christ whom you have sent" (17:3). The word *know* means to "realize through experience." Eternal life isn't just about life after death—it's about knowing God by experience right now!

As we come to know God, He gives us His heart for the world and we become His Kingdom ambassadors. Not only is our purpose to know Him, we are here to make Him known. That is why we should pray, "Your Kingdom come, Your will be done." Our desire is for God's glory to fill the earth, for His Kingdom to come, that everyone everywhere may know Him. This "Kingdom come" way of life leads us to live with purpose. We're not just looking to God to rescue us from hellfire and brimstone; we're laying down our lives for the purpose of making Jesus famous in the world, asking that His will be done. We have freely received; now we are invited to partner with God to "freely give" (Matthew 10:7-8). The King has placed us here on assignment. We are on mission.

– Questions to Consider –

• How comfortable are you with the idea of simply *being with* God? Why do we often feel we must *do* something *for* God?

• How are God's glory and your life's purpose related? How do you feel about spending your life for God's glory?

30
Mission Debriefing

When it comes to partnering with God in His mission, it is helpful to think of it in two parts: general assignment and specific assignment.[4] We all share the same general assignment of knowing God and making Him known. We are tasked with the privilege and responsibility, as God's ambassadors, to make sure our neighbors, friends, and family have had opportunity to hear the good news about Jesus and His Kingdom. But each of us also has a specific assignment—a distinct way of fulfilling this general assignment in our own particular context.

For some, this specific assignment may be to play and write music that reveals beauty and draws people to the heart of God. Others are called to lead businesses and create revenue that is used to provide for under-resourced individuals and families or improve living conditions around the world. Others will bring God glory in their art. Still others may fulfill God's purposes by flying an airplane or repairing cars. Ephesians 2:10 tells us we are God's special creation, works of art, recreated in Christ with a unique destiny to fulfill and specific works to accomplish.[5] These good works, which God designed for us ahead of time, will look different from person to person, but all serve to accomplish God's overarching purpose of filling the earth with His glory that we might come to know Him.

[4] For more on this concept, see Rick Warren's book The Purpose-Driven Life.
[5] See specifically The Passion Translation.

Of course, this begs the question, *How do we know what our specific assignment is?* How do we discover the unique calling God has for our lives? A good first step in answering most questions is to ask more questions. In this case, asking reflective questions can help us understand our specific assignment. *Who am I? What can I do? What am I passionate about? Where do I fit?* As we live and serve and learn, we will pick up clues along the way that lead to a greater understanding of the distinct role we were designed to play.

The first question is the question of identity: *Who am I?* Next to understanding who God is, understanding who we are is the most important lesson we will ever learn. If we never realize who we were made to be, we may spend our entire lives trying to be someone else and miss out on the good works for which God designed us. What a tragedy! Bill Johnson, pastor and author, once said, "When you know who God has made you to be, you won't want to be anyone else!" The truth is we realize our true identity only by hearing what God says about us. As we read Scripture, spend time talking with God, and listen for what He is saying through people and circumstances, we come to understand more clearly what God says about us. This is what ultimately defines us, not what our teachers or families or even closest friends say. Who better to listen to than the one who through His words spoke the universe into existence?

Understanding what God says about us is the first step, but it's also important to realize how each of us are uniquely designed. In His sovereignty, God has made each of us a unique expression of His divine fingerprint. It doesn't take long to look around and see that each of us is different! What makes one person laugh differs with what someone else finds funny. Some like things orderly and organized; others couldn't care less. Some seek safety while others seek adventure. God doesn't make carbon copies; He makes custom masterpieces (Ephesians 2:10; Psalm 139). It's important then for us to learn what makes us different. Are you loud and outspoken or quiet and reserved? Would you prefer a night out with a large crowd of people or an evening alone with a good book? Do you make decisions based on facts or on how you feel?

Meditating on God's words about us and understanding our unique, God-given design go a long way in giving us insight into who we are. As we discover *how* we were made it will become clearer *why* we were made.

– Questions to Consider –

• What's the difference between general assignment and specific assignment? What is our general assignment?

• How would you describe your personality to a friend? Use at least three descriptive words. How might God use these qualities for His glory?

31
Abilities & Desires

As we discover our identity through what God says about us and understanding how we were made, another important question to consider is, *What can I do? What skills and giftings do I have? What is it that I do well? Skills* are "abilities that have been acquired through training, practice, or life experience" (*Merriam-Webster.com*).

Bill can build houses, Sue can paint cars, Don can work on computers—these are all skills that have been developed over time and can be used for God's glory. God's plan will always take us beyond our level of expertise (He doesn't just want us to do what *we* can do; He wants us to do what only *He* can do) but knowing what we can do is still a good place to start. For example, if someone's house burns down and you are a carpenter, God may call you to do more than just pray for the person—He may call you to use your skills to help build a new house.

While skills are abilities acquired over time, giftings are abilities that come natural to us. Gifts are still to be honed and developed, but they are abilities that may come easier to some than to others. There are some born with a knack for athletics. Others are born with beautiful voices. Still others are naturally poetic and, with the right meter and rhyme, could make Monday-morning traffic sound appealing. Then there are the spiritual giftings mentioned in the previous section, given by the Holy Spirit for the building up of the

Church. Discovering these skills and abilities helps us better understand who we are and what we were made to do.

A final question to evaluate is, *What am I passionate about?* Passion has to do with dreams and desires. It's what wakes us up in the morning and keeps us dreaming at night. It's what motivates us to keep trying, keep working, and keep pressing on when we hit hard times. If we're not sure what we are passionate about, we can ask ourselves these questions: *What angers me? What excites me? What saddens me? If I could change anything in the world, what would I change?* Answering these questions gives us insight into our passions. They give us insight into what we are committed to and what we value.

As we discover our passions, it is important to realize that God is *for* our desires. Scripture says that as we enjoy God, He gives us the desires of our heart (Psalm 37:4). The truth is, God wants to give you what you want! Often we must wait and sometimes we get a "no" or "not now," but God only withholds from us that which would hurt us rather than help us (Romans 8:32). God wants us to have dreams and desires, but He doesn't want them to have us! Aside from sinful, selfish desires, we can trust that God is actually the one who puts desires in our hearts. We ultimately surrender our dreams and desires to God in order to follow Him fully, but often He wants to use those implanted passions and desires for His purpose. The thing we are most passionate about may just be our God-given assignment!

God has custom-crafted each of us in a way that fits with His purpose and design. He has given us special interests, unique skills and abilities, and desires that align with His heart as we seek Him. As we offer these back to God for His purposes, He invites us to partner with Him in His mission to redeem and restore the world.

— Questions to Consider —

• What special giftings and skills have you developed over the years? How might God use these to bless the world?

• What is something you would like to see change in the world? How might God use you to bring about that change? In what ways could you begin to dream bigger?

32
Finding Your Place

While it is important for each of us to take time to ponder questions of assignment and identity and to realize our skills and abilities, this can't be done in isolation. The best way to learn where we fit and how we can partner with God is to find a people, find a place, and start serving. Rather than demanding we do something we feel aligns with our gifting and design, we should look around and recognize the needs and opportunities before us and get involved! God often uses the opportunities that could easily be overlooked to shape us into the people He wants us to be and to do the good works He wants us to do.

A young person may believe he was created to act on the big screen or declare God's glory from a stage, but he may need to serve God by faithfully stacking chairs week in and week out before he ever sets foot on a stage. It is in the context of service that we grow in understanding of God's assignment for us and our character is grown to match the opportunities that will come our way.

The truth is, opportunities to partner with God are all around us, but we too often don't recognize them as such. They usually present themselves disguised as needs and a lot of hard work. If we're looking for rock-star status or a way to advance our own agenda, we won't be able to see the real opportunities right in front of us. Instead we need to ask ourselves: *What needs are there in my community? In what ways could I serve my church and family and friends? Is there anything that should be done but is left undone because no one is willing or able to do it?* As we answer these questions we find there are plenty of opportunities to serve right where we are! If we are looking to love Jesus and expand His Kingdom and are willing to serve, there will never be a shortage of opportunities.

If there are multiple opportunities before us and any one of them would be a great way to serve God and love people, we should consider chemistry (no, not the table of elements and bubbling beakers). Chemistry is how well a person "fits" in a given situation or with a group of people. Just as a puzzle is made up of varying pieces designed to fit together in a specific way to form the complete picture, there is an ideal fit for each of us in our areas of service. For example, a woman may see an opportunity to serve God both on the worship team and in the maintenance department. Both opportunities are real areas of need. But this woman has never been able to carry a tune and has never played an instrument, nor is she interested in putting in the many of hours of practice required to learn. She does, however, enjoy working with her hands and has some experience in basic handiwork. Clearly, one of these opportunities is a better fit than the other.

When more than one opportunity is before us, we should consider our assignment and our design. *Which opportunity most fits my skill set? Which opportunity interests me most and aligns with my desires? Could I do this joyfully?*[6] *What is God calling me to do?*

Along with considering what we are to do, we must also consider the people with whom we will serve. Looking at Scripture we find that great men and women of God rarely worked alone. Jesus traveled with and worked alongside

---

[6] You can do most anything joyfully if you so choose. However, choosing joy is easier in some opportunities than others.

twelve other men. He was often accompanied by several women who took care of the group's logistical needs (Luke 8:1-3). Jesus' followers didn't always know what they'd be doing but they knew whom they would be with. Jesus sent the disciples out to preach the Gospel two by two. The apostle Paul didn't travel alone. He had dozens of travel companions as he preached the Gospel around the world, many of whom traveled with him for years at a time. The point is God doesn't just call us to a work, He calls us to a people. Consider: *Who am I called to follow? Who am I called to lead? Do we get along? Do we share like passions and vision? Am I willing to submit when I disagree?*

As we come to understand who God has made us to be with our unique temperament, skills, and desires, and have explored the needs and opportunities before us, it's time to get involved. Commit to serve, commit to community, and join Jesus on His mission to bring the Kingdom of Heaven here to earth.

– Questions to Consider –

• What needs do you see around you? What opportunities? How might God use you to meet these needs?

• Who might God be calling you to serve with? Are you ready to commit to a particular team/area of service? What would prepare you to make that commitment?

– Application Exercise –
Personality Assessment & Getting Connected

Complete a personality assessment and review the results with your coach. You can complete a free Myers-Briggs Personality Assessment online at *16personalities. com* or the DISC assessment for free at *123test.com/disc-personality-test/*

Ask a friend or pastor about ways to get connected and to serve at your local church, then get involved!

Conclusion

You did it! Your journey through this book is complete. What now? My hope is that these chapters, questions, and exercises have challenged and inspired you to continue journeying onward with Jesus and other Jesus-followers. God's Kingdom is ever advancing and He wants you and me to be a part. This venture is not for the fainthearted, but He says we can do it. All we have to do is take the next step. We've read a bit about the Kingdom and what it means to journey with Jesus. Now the challenge is to continue walking. To take the next step . . . and the next . . . and the next. Continue moving deeper into relationship with your loving Father, resist the devil, discipline yourself for godliness, and use your giftings to serve others and build up the Church for the glory of God.

And remember, the Kingdom is a Person, not a place. We seek what we cannot see. But as we spend time with our heavenly Father, we hear His Holy Spirit speak to us; and by considering love's response we learn to follow well. We keep watching, listening, and submitting to our Father-King and His fruit grows in us and we are made like Him.

But the Kingdom is not just a Person, it is a people. It is His Church. Jesus has chosen to delegate His authority through us! All who follow Him and are in relationship with Him as sons and daughters now carry the Kingdom. We are outposts spread across this planet. Where we go, the Kingdom goes.

A great next step after reading this book is to get plugged into a committed group of believers who pray, worship, study the Bible, and share the message of Jesus with others. If you are not part of a healthy local church, I strongly encourage you to start asking for God's guidance about where to get involved. If you read this book with a friend or a coach, ask them for a recommendation on healthy and thriving churches in your area. No church is perfect. No pastor or leadership team is perfect. No structure is perfect. The Church is full of sinful, messy people who have been brought in, transformed by grace, and now live as sons and daughters of the King. But this imperfect Church is the means by which God wants to restore the world to relationship with Himself. City by city. Village by village. And nation by nation.

Get involved. Engage in authentic community. Serve wholeheartedly. Love courageously. Submit yourself to other believers. Be a part of God's activity in the world today.

Together, as we obey Jesus' teachings to love God and love people, we will find ourselves discovering a joy previously unknown to us. We will live an adventure, following Jesus in this Kingdom way of life. Step by step. May we come to know Him along the way, and may we live lives that boldly declare:

Our Father in Heaven,
Let Your name be kept holy.
Your Kingdom come,
Your will be done,
On earth as it is in Heaven. Amen.

A Prayer for Forgiveness

Father God,

I come to You aware of my own sin and brokenness. I confess that I have sinned against You and ask that You bring all hidden things into Your light [you may want to speak out specific sins and sinful patterns with which you have partnered]. *I take responsibility for the wrong choices I have made and for the pain it has brought about in my life and the lives of those around me.*

I renounce this sin [state specific thoughts, behaviors, patterns, etc.] *and the place I have given it in my life. I break the partnering agreement I have knowingly or unknowingly made with this sin and ask that You send this sin and any related demonic influences away from me never to return.*

Father, I thank You for sending Your Son, Jesus, as the perfect payment for my sin. I receive complete forgiveness and my Father's favor on the basis of Jesus' death and resurrection. I stand before you now clean and accepted, forgiven and free, restored to right relationship with You.

I receive the gift of the Holy Spirit and ask that You fill me with Your Spirit and every good thing You have stored up for me today [ask God what He wants to give you].

Thank You for Your grace and mercy! Amen.

Recommended Resources

Nothing Hidden Ministries
- *nothinghidden.com*
- Specifically, the *NHM Tool Booklet*

The Alpha Course
- *alphausa.org*

Heart of the Father Ministries
- *heartofthefather.com*
- Specifically, *Unbound* by Neal Lozano

Ransomed Heart Ministries
- *ransomedheart.com/pray*
- Specifically, daily prayer PDFs

The Purpose Driven Life by Rick Warren
- *purposedriven.com*

Emotionally Healthy Discipleship
- *emotionallyhealthy.org*
- Specifically, *Emotionally Healthy Spirituality* by Peter Scazzero

The Bible Project
- *thebibleproject.com*